THE
QUALITY-PRODUCTIVITY
CONNECTION
in service-sector
management

This Book Is Dedicated To

Robert Beyer

Donald W. Jennings

and

Robert Trueblood

my late partners who taught me so much
about the meaning of service.

THE
QUALITY-PRODUCTIVITY
CONNECTION
in service-sector
management

By JOHN C. SHAW, CPA
Partner
Touche Ross & Co.

 VAN NOSTRAND REINHOLD COMPANY
NEW YORK   CINCINNATI   ATLANTA   DALLAS   SAN FRANCISCO
LONDON   TORONTO   MELBOURNE

Van Nostrand Reinhold Company Regional Offices:
New York   Cincinnati   Atlanta   Dallas   San Francisco

Van Nostrand Reinhold Company International Offices:
London   Toronto   Melbourne

Library of Congress Catalog Card Number: 78-15756
ISBN: 0-442-27542-0

Manufactured in the United States of America

Published by Van Nostrand Reinhold Company
135 West 50th Street, New York, N. Y. 10020

Published simultaneously in Canada by Van Nostrand Reinhold Ltd.

15   14   13   12   11   10   9   8   7   6   5   4   3   2   1

Library of Congress Cataloging in Publication Data

Shaw, John Clark, 1933-
    The quality-productivity connection in service-sector
management.

    Includes index.
    1. Management.   I. Title.
HD31.S434   658.4   78-15756
ISBN 0-442-27542-0

CONTENTS

FOREWORD

This book brings both recognition and constructive thought to bear on some of the most critical, bedrock issues facing the United States today:

- Can free enterprise survive in a world which is becoming more socialistic in some quarters, more despotic in others?

- Can the United States maintain its role of world leadership, or is a decline as inevitable for us as it has been for other dominant nations throughout history?

- If it is to retain a role of leadership, can the United States make the transition successfully from an economy dominated by manufacturing to a service economy without greatly increased government intervention or ultimate domination by big government?

These, I submit, are questions of survival – survival for an economic system and a way of life which have been held virtually sacred. Without detailing our history, it is safe to say that the United States was catapulted to a position of economic predominance by the thrust of the industrial revolution, a thrust fueled by abundant resources.

We have been so accustomed to thinking of ourselves in terms of industrial might that the transition to a service economy status occurred with little or no fanfare or even recognition by management generally. Again, it would be pointless to retrace history. It is enough to establish that a clear majority of the U.S. economy falls within the service sector.

The timing of this development coincides with some other trends of potentially catastrophic proportions. One is the continuing energy crisis and its expansion into other areas of resource shortages. Another is the maturing of the post-World War II baby boom, creating a condition of at least temporary labor oversupply and attendant unemployment. On still another front, we appear to be suffering from our own affluence as continuing inflation drives our products off world markets while discontent apparently continues to fester in our labor force.

In this book, my partner, Jack Shaw, takes an intelligent and realistic look at the management issues and challenges which have to be met if U.S. managers are to succeed, individually and collectively, in managing one of the world's few free-enterprise service economies.

Mr. Shaw reviews the challenges associated with such a goal. He concludes that service entities in both the private and public sectors can survive and even prosper. To do so, however, managers will have to recognize that time-proven management approaches and techniques will not do the job anymore in the changed environment that confronts them. New systems of management are necessary for today's service enterprises. This book presents and describes such a new system.

Jack Shaw sees new and exciting challenges open for managers willing to make a commitment to quality of service. Particularly noteworthy is that the opportunities and challenges are seen as existing across the whole spectrum of our economy, encompassing the public sector as well as private industry.

This is an important reality to be recognized. The day is gone – or soon will be – when bureaucrats can sit in judgment over our private lives and private businesses as critical spectator, judge, and jury. It is becoming apparent that government itself is a business, with all of the responsibilities and accountabilities this status implies. People are not buying the inevitability of increasing governmental costs and declining quality and productivity of services anymore. They are becoming mad, perhaps mad enough to stimulate responsiveness and turnaround.

Jack Shaw holds, in an early chapter, that we should expect the same standards of quality of service from all entities which provide them – public or private. He maintains that government agencies cannot effectively mandate or legislate quality standards which they do not understand and cannot emulate themselves. This book maintains that all service entities – governmental as well as private – should be managed for responsiveness to their markets and market conditions. If they are, according to Jack Shaw, improved productivity will be realized and greater profitability will result.

This is a thought-provoking work which could start a trend in management. Let us hope it does.

Russell E. Palmer, CPA
Managing Partner and
  Chief Executive Officer
Touche Ross & Co.

PREFACE

One of the many unique aspects of practical management is that practice frequently precedes theory. Problem solving leads almost simultaneously to both theoretical and operational breakthroughs. Significant improvements stem from insights born of firing-line pressures.

This work is about the results of such an experience. The insight came from studies and consulting engagements covering a wide range of service entities:

A direct connection should exist between the quality of services delivered (measured in terms of customer satisfaction) and productivity realized. The connection is straightforward: *where management policy provides for a direct connection between quality and productivity, profitability will result.*

In examining the relationship between quality and productivity, it also became apparent that the same set of management policies which promotes quality also assures productivity. These policies must be an integral part of an organization's strategies and plans.

Although these principles are easily stated, the formulation of successful strategies remains unique to each individual service entity. No attempt is made to tell the reader how to formulate winning competitive policies. Rather, requirements for and results of such elements of successful management are stated. Then a general-purpose system of management for implementing successful competitive policies is described.

Such a system of management is built largely by recombining proven theories, principles, and techniques. Thus, there is no detailed description of methods which are already well known. Rather, a practical approach to organizing, managing, and operating a service enterprise for competitive success is put forward.

Success is the central theme. The successes described have been both observed and created. Concentration is on the lessons to be derived from successful – rather than unsuccessful – enterprises. An analogy can be drawn to illustrate this approach and its effects: it is as though a medical team interested in health studied patients who are well rather than concentrating, as is traditionally done, on those who are ill.

In business, experience has shown that there is much more to be learned from success than from failure. Analyses of failures cannot produce much more than conjecture about causes. Once a company has failed, it becomes extremely difficult to prove what would have happened if different courses had been followed. Success, however, delivers its own proof of soundness. Lessons derived from success can be followed with some degree of assurance.

Therefore, this work isolates and shows how to emulate specific areas of success dealing with competition through policies which assure quality and productivity for service entities. If quality and productivity are realized, it is felt, profitability cannot be far behind.

With this orientation, the audience to whom this book is directed is readily identifiable: the primary reader is an active, decision-level executive of a service enterprise. Also targeted as readers are managers at all levels responsible for implementing management policies within service organizations.

An attempt has been made to bring perspective and, hopefully, some order into a maze of conflicting theories and advice to which these managers may have been subjected. In their efforts to cope with increases in both costs and customer dissatisfaction with the hassles involved in acquiring services, service-sector managers have been bombarded by behaviorists on the one hand and hard-nosed operational advisers on the other. The behaviorists talk in terms of changing employee expectations and the need for increased sensitivity. The operational people keep hammering on the theme of increasing productivity through volume processing techniques to improve bottom-line results. The system of management proposed here is intended as a tool for doing something about this kind of quandary by solving both quality and productivity problems with a single management system.

It is also felt that this book may have some value as a supplementary text for graduate or upper undergraduate business school students. For such students, the ideas presented can provide an understanding of the common denominators between organizational development concepts on the one hand and operational management considerations on the other. I believe these seemingly conflicting areas have been blended into a single approach to management which is understandable and teachable.

This book represents a compilation of learning experiences which span many scores of consulting engagements conducted in cooperation with people who are just too numerous to name individually. However, a few specific contributions have been too valuable to omit:

Robert White, Executive Vice President, and Barry Young, Senior Vice President, both with the Service Management Group of Citibank, have been close collaborators in the development and implementation of many of the ideas put forward.

A number of my partners, particularly Dave Moxley, Max Sporer, Donald Curtis, and Arnold Ditri, have provided invaluable sounding boards and professional contributions. Ram Capoor, a senior consultant on my staff in New York, also spent considerable effort helping to formulate our concepts.

Important theoretical and conceptual inputs and checkpointing have been realized in extensive conversations with three professors of the Harvard Business School: Robert N. Anthony, Jay W. Lorsch, and Anthony Athos.

Donald Trawicki, one of my partners and co-author of the book, *Profitability Accounting,* provided thoughtful insight into the process of management control.

September, 1978   John C. Shaw

1
THE
INSIGHT

WHY ARE SOME COMPANIES PERENNIAL WINNERS?

Have you ever wondered why some companies appear to be consistently more successful than their competitors?

Why are other companies shooting stars on the business scene?

Some companies seem to have success in their corporate genes. Long after they have come up with a big innovation which has been copied by everybody else, they still dominate their markets. They are still regarded as the Cadillacs in their particular field. Winning is a way with them.

By contrast, other firms seem to run a short winning streak, then fade. We say they ride a trend or that they capitalize on a momentary opportunity. They don't have staying power. They are not winners in the long run.

I like to think that some companies have the genetic properties to make them world-class competitors. They perform again and again. I think of them as superb athletes. I have also found it worthwhile, in evaluating organizations and their potential, to think seriously about what makes them that way.

WHAT DOES A WINNER LOOK LIKE?

Among athletes, the characteristics of superb performance identify themselves pretty readily: strength, speed, peripheral vision, instincts, desire, drive, and persistence. Winning companies and their competitive characteristics are also readily identifiable.

The winning ways of Merrill Lynch & Co. stand out largely because of the high rate of attrition which has taken place among competitors. In the investment-banking field, most other firms have had to merge to survive. Merrill Lynch, on the other hand, set itself up as a winner through early identification of a need for a retail distribution network and through innovative, adaptive management to capitalize on this network in delivering services.

State Farm Insurance has built a dominant position in a competitive industry by recognizing a market need and devising a better way to meet it. In 1922, founder George J. Mecherle, a farmer himself, noted from statistics that farmers were experiencing a lower rate of auto accidents than urban drivers. Studying the needs of this market, Mecherle devised a new way to serve it, through independent agents representing his firm exclusively. The company has built a network of independent agents who have become the highest earners in the industry as State Farm has become one of the world's largest and most successful insurance companies.

You can also look to examples as everyday as the common hamburger. McDonald's never tells the world they make a tasty hamburger. They do tell their people and their marketplace that they offer excellent service, clean surroundings, and good value. Their emphasis on quality has also carried them to a dominant position of productivity, as announced on their own scoreboards showing how many billions of hamburgers they have sold.

IBM has never presented itself as a computer manufacturer. The company and its people see themselves as being in the problem-solving and decision-supporting business. They sell applications and the value of the results of those applications. They do so with considerable pride and spirit, traits which they see as separating them from the rest of the office equipment industry. They have been consistent winners because the same pride and quality consciousness have characterized the organization for more than 60 years. Demonstrating that these are the traits behind consistent winning, IBM has moved successfully into fields dominated by others, including dictation, copying, communication, and word processing equipment.

Winning doesn't always have to be spectacular. Look at United Parcel Service. Even to a casual observer, here's a company which projects a steady image of a cleanly washed truck performing dependably. Efficient delivery people get packages across the country faster and less expensively than the Postal Service. They perform just as dependably in the same town or across the street, as one department store after another has testified in discontinuing its own delivery services in favor of UPS.

The past three or four decades have seen a proliferation of computer service bureaus and payroll services of one description or another. Through it all, Automatic Data Processing (ADP) has consistently built an image for delivering error-free accounting and payroll services on a nationwide basis – reliably and with substantial profits. Quality and productivity have been teammates in the ADP scheme of things.

WHAT MAKES A WORLD-CLASS COMPETITOR?

Championship is in the genes. If you'll pardon the analogy between biological and organizational systems, the fact remains that a world-class athlete has exceptional, inborn traits. With an organization, the necessary drive and stamina have to be implanted through management.

The underlying truth is that, over the long run, businesses really compete through management policies which concentrate on relating quality of services rendered (as perceived by customers) with the productivity of the people delivering those services.

WHY ARE QUALITY-PRODUCTIVITY POLICIES MORE IMPORTANT TO WINNING THAN OTHER MANAGEMENT POLICIES?

Note that this question about management policy applies specifically to the ability of an organization to compete. No other aspects of management or organizational success are being addressed within the context of this work or of the system of management it advocates. Given this framework, it is easy to illustrate how policies directed toward quality of service and productivity of people have a greater impact on competitive service than other areas of management.

Consider, for example, the area of new products or services. Innovation, in itself, has an indisputable impact on an enterprise's competitive position. But this impact tends to be short-lived because innovations – particularly in services – can be readily and quickly copied. Thus, the advantage of innovation lasts only as long as it takes competitors to provide the same service under a different name, possibly with different gimmicks.

The short duration of innovation holds particularly true in a service environment. In manufacturing, distribution, or agriculture, capital-formation and technological-development requirements can inhibit attempts to replicate the products of competitors. But, where services are concerned, lead times for product development can be short and the cost of entry, in terms of capital, tends to be low.

As an example, consider the innovative decision to serve breakfast at McDonald's outlets. Added capital and technology were not significant factors. A short-term competitive edge was realized. But the competition followed suit within weeks or months. In the long run, McDonald's success rests upon a more lasting set of policies which establish standards for quality and productivity. Breakfast service results in improvements in both these areas; customer services are increased while productivity of both people and facilities is expanded.

The same kind of factors have been at work in commercial banking. A few years ago, this industry experienced a number of rapidly copied innovations: consolidated customer statements, new uses for credit cards, automatic bill paying, overdraft loans against checking accounts, and others. Time proved, however, that lasting success in banking derived from identifying and serving needs of customer groups on a quality basis rather than from the rush into new products or services.

New products and services do, of course, impact competition. But they tend to produce temporary surges rather than lasting results. By comparison, a dedication to quality of service and related productivity does more to sustain long-term competitive success.

Another competitive factor impacted by management decisions is pricing. Lower prices, loss leaders, or even giveaways, do effect competitive positions, but only temporarily. Certainly, price reductions are competitive acts which are easily followed. However, no matter how attractive the price of a product or service, there is no level at which unsatisfactory services can be justified.

Pricing policies alone cannot assure success. For evidence, consider the experience at GEICO, the Government Employees Insurance Company. Despite an extremely competitive pricing structure, this company nearly failed. If the fortunes of this organization are turned around, this won't happen because of pricing. The point: pricing advantages alone will not give a company the staying power of a champion.

Capital formation is important for competition in some industries. Certainly, it can be said that a number of successful financial, real estate, manufacturing, and distribution organizations support their success through management of capital resources.

However, this factor is not as critical in service areas as elsewhere. Though a service organization must be adequately capitalized, the availability of funds can be more of a result than a cause of competitive success. It seems apparent, for example, that once the concept of McDonald's approach to its marketplace was proven, capital was not an issue. Neither was money a critical factor in the initial success of this organization.

There are those who say that success of a service enterprise is all about location. The old saying is that the three most important requirements for a retail store, hotel, or restaurant are: location, location, and location.

Location is indeed vital – as long as all other factors which drive a business are equal among competitors. It is not hard to illustrate, however, that quality of service to identified, targeted customers can override even the location factor: another major department store outlet failed in a location just a few blocks from Bloomingdale's. As a further illustration, Macy's turned around a declining situation at its 34th Street location in Manhattan by enhancing the quality of goods and services offered, as seen from the viewpoint of customers in that area.

There is no intent to downplay the importance of location. Rather, the idea is that quality service to a specific, targeted portion of the marketplace can be far more important to competitive success.

Personnel policies are also emerging as an important management element. Convincing evidence is being put forward to indicate that participative personnel policies contribute to the success of service enterprises.

If a customer-service policy has not been established, however, no amount of personnel involvement can lead to competitive success. This is illustrated in our public schools. These institutions have about as much employee participation as is possible. But these practices have not secured success, as evidenced by test scores of students and evaluations of many parents.

Management theory or science is another frequently cited factor for competitive success. But even the most scientific approach to running a business can be misapplied if the enterprise itself is not in tune with its marketplace. This is particularly true where management theories or techniques have been borrowed from one sector and transferred bodily into the service area. No matter how sound the theory, competitive success cannot be impacted unless customers can be convinced the company is oriented to serve their needs.

For lasting competitive success in a service endeavor, I am convinced that the driving force lies in adopting and implementing policies which gear an organization to deliver quality services. These same policies, experience has shown, can also serve to enhance productivity realized in the delivery of services.

WHAT DO THESE POLICIES LOOK LIKE?

Symbolically, the policy relationship between quality and productivity can be expressed as is shown in Figure 1-1. As this illustration indicates, the starting key in formulating a baseline competitive policy is to recognize the direct relationship which can exist between quality and productivity. Once this relationship is established firmly, profitability results.

The characteristics of a policy expressing the quality-productivity connection are diagrammed in Figure 1-2. This illustration emphasizes that the quality and productivity elements of management policy are formulated and applied in parallel. There can be a temptation to see a cause-effect relationship between quality and productivity. In some cases, such a relationship may, in fact, exist. But in formulating management policy, the two elements should be treated as parallel components.

On the quality side, the first characteristic listed stresses that quality must be judged from the customer's perception. In doing this, a partnership between customer and provider unique to the rendering of a service should be recognized. Identification of this customer-provider relationship is an insight stated by Herbert Heaton in his book, *Productivity in Service Organizations*.

The parallel characteristic on the productivity side establishes that the provider should have a sensitivity to customer needs. Such a sensitivity should be achieved by each individual employee level within the service enterprise through establishment of a client-type relationship between the deliverer of services and the consumer. Productivity is enhanced through recognition that the provider is in a partnership relationship with the customer.

The second characteristic of service quality is that an almost infinite variability can exist in delivered services. That is, it could conceivably be possible that each customer applies a different perception to every service utilized, *every time the customer and provider come into contact*. Thus, the full scope of services could build to a combined total equaling the number of customers multiplied by the number of services offered, then multiplied again by the number of opportunities presented. There also should be recognition that each service transaction is individual and unique because of the personal interaction between the customer and the deliverer.

The productivity counterpart for the second characteristic is that employees who deliver services should have a reasonably broad scope of responsibility and the discretion to take the actions necessary to assure customer satisfaction at each encounter. This means that each individual rendering services should have sufficient breadth of knowledge and capabilities to meet customer needs for service variability with a degree of independence.

The third quality characteristic is value. This value should be judged in terms of the customer's perception of the relationship between expectations and costs. Values too have a variability. Each customer has a preconception of what he or she should receive for the expense incurred.

The productivity parallel for value lies in unit cost. This reflects the efficiency and effectiveness with which customer expectations are met.

The final characteristic, or ingredient, for quality is warranty. A quality commitment means the supplier stands behind products or services. Warranty assures customers that the supplier will make things right if anything goes wrong. It also implies that the provider will be interested in the customer's satisfaction, even when things are going right.

The productivity parallel for warranty lies in the personal pride and satisfaction which people should feel as a result of having delivered quality services effectively and efficiently.

These are the characteristics of a single, integrated policy relating quality and productivity to build the competitive posture of an organization. As each manager formulates and applies the quality-productivity connection to his or her own company, measures should be taken to communicate these policy elements throughout the service organization as an integral set. If this is done, management action will, in turn, stimulate a set of attitudes and behaviors which are incorporated into the basic fabric and culture of the business. Marvin Bower of McKinsey & Company describes a policy which has been communicated and understood as "the way we do things around here."

Once such a baseline competitive policy is in place, it is extremely difficult for competitors to copy because it represents a set of attitudes and behaviors which comprise an organizational state of mind. This is far more difficult to replicate than any individual product or service, no matter how competitive.

HOW DOES THIS POLICY AFFECT COMPETITIVE CAPABILITIES?

Policies don't deliver services. Policies also do not compete. Organizations of people do. Thus, policies have no impact or value until they are implemented. The real issue, I submit, lies in implementation of policies for competitive success.

This implementation is facilitated by an integrated system of management which is inherently sound and universally understood within the organization. Such an integrated system is made up of many components and applies many principles. Most discussions about management methods or techniques tend to focus upon a single principle at the expense of others. I believe it is more effective to apply a balanced set of principles and techniques in a single, unified system of management designed to assure competitive success.

On their own, none of the individual components of a successful system of management may be unique or innovative. Actually, the approach recommended in subsequent chapters consists largely of a collection of proven, off-the-shelf techniques. While none of these is new or startling in itself, the overall effect is to assure implementation of policies which reflect the competitive differences between businesses.

Thus, a policy relating quality and productivity affects the competitive capabilities of an organization by providing a framework within which the entity can be managed for competitive success.

WHERE DOES THIS LEAVE US?

By inference and example, this discussion has supported a conclusion that there is a direct relationship between the quality of services a business renders to its customers and the productivity of its people. Further, it has been established that the same set of management policies developed to assure quality also lead to enhanced productivity. It follows that high levels of quality and productivity can be expected to lead to profitability for the enterprise.

The setting of policies and strategies which govern the very culture and beliefs of an organization is a highly individualized, unique process. It remains a challenge for individual managers to work out such policies for their own companies. The only help which can be offered is to indicate that a dedication to customer satisfaction – as perceived from the customer's own viewpoint – is an essential ingredient for such a set of policies.

Once an understanding of these principles and an appropriate set of policies are in place within a company, it is possible to apply a uniform, general-purpose system of management to implement those policies. Such a system of management has been devised and is presented in later chapters.

WHERE DO WE GO FROM HERE?

The entire principle of the quality-productivity connection and its potential for profitability rests on an awareness of the expectations of an organization's customers. Thus, an understanding of both the frustrations and rewards associated with the delivery of services to customers is our next logical topic. This is covered in Chapter 2.

$$Q \cup P - P_1$$

Where:

Q   =   Quality as perceived by the customer

P   =   Productivity as reflected in employee output

P_1 =   Profitability

Legend:

When quality and productivity are related, profitability results.

Figure 1-1

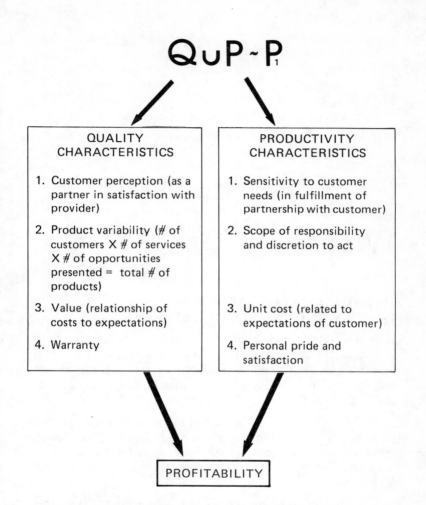

Elements of a policy reflecting the quality-productivity connection.

Figure 1-2

2
WHY?

WHY THE CONCERN ABOUT QUALITY AND PRODUCTIVITY?

It is not the purpose or intent of this book to hang crepe on America. Too many people have tried that already. There is no need for yet another comparison between trends in this country and the post-industrial declines in Great Britain, France, Italy, and elsewhere.

However, there is a need to look realistically at obvious problems which do exist – and to look behind them for the opportunities they generate. All consumers of services – which is to say everyone – experience daily frustrations, particularly with quality.

Reviewing these frustrations can help managers build their own understanding of how customers perceive their services. Adopting the customer's viewpoint, in turn, can lead to insights into how policies relating quality and productivity can reduce frustrations and improve satisfaction for consumers while enhancing profitability for the provider of services. Basically, people and organizations want to deal with suppliers of services who deliver frustration-free satisfaction.

Many executives are not personally aware of the kinds of frustrations experienced by their publics or customers. Most top-level managers are able to shield themselves from these frustrations through their relative affluence. For example, in our major cities, few top executives experience the aggravations and fears of inadequate and potentially unsafe public transportation at night. When they or members of their families need health-care attention, they do not wait in line at clinics. If educational quality becomes a problem, they can solve it by enrolling their children in private schools.

The list could be virtually endless. The point is concise: in setting management policies dealing with quality and productivity, it is necessary to stand in the shoes of the prospective customer. The delivery system for services should be examined from the outside looking in. This should be done with empathy for the consumer or recipient of services.

This situation and the need for dealing with it have been articulated well by Edward B. Rust, President of State Farm Insurance Companies: "The tendency is to encapsulate oneself in corporate limousines and executive suites and paneled boardrooms – an environment that in the long run will distort management's view of reality. It's entirely human and understandable, I suspect, that most of us seek to make our lives more comfortable, to escape in some measure the harsh realities of human existence.

"But I suggest to you that it is an inescapable part of the businessman's job to maintain direct personal touch with the realities of the marketplace. Market research is fine and necessary – but those neat charts and graphs can never give you the feel of product and user that you get from a direct confrontation with an angry or happy customer."

WHAT ARE OUR SERVICE FRUSTRATIONS?

Perhaps the most marked frustration with services lies in the feeling that personal contact – and personal caring – have been lost. Day after day, we are struck by the depersonalization of services. Our telephone calls are answered by machines. Our correspondence is answered by computer-produced form letters. We transact financial business with an automated teller machine. We tend to resign ourselves to learning that airline or hotel reservations have been fouled up. When things go wrong, we expect people to blame a computer. We find it increasingly hard to establish a personal, or client, type of relationship around the delivery of services. We seem to have lost a sense of personal responsibility for the outcomes of our own efforts in the delivery of services.

The Hassle Factor

No thinking person is really serious about wanting to return to the good old days. Anyone who lived through them will admit that the old days weren't really all that good. On the other hand, today's depersonalization leads to a deterioration in the quality of life which can be described as a "hassle." The hassle factor makes it hard to get things done.

In any major city, for example, people condition themselves to carry pocketfuls of change, small bills, or credit cards to satisfy the demands of increasing numbers of machines and exact-change rules. If we forget any of these new necessities of urban life, we may well be unable to ride the bus, use the telephone, or buy gasoline for our cars in certain areas.

For both individuals and businesses, masses of paperwork and red tape must be endured. This is particularly true in the relationships between government and businesses. As it becomes more and more of a hassle to interact with our environment, the cost and ultimate quality of services suffer unavoidably.

Inflation

One of the frustrations which has existed throughout the lifetime of most of today's managers has been inflation. On one side, there is the fear that it will be impossible to pass along all of the increased costs which are experienced. This can result in reduced margins of profitability and viability – particularly for small businesses.

The other side of the dual impact of inflation lies in the changes caused in the expectations and attitudes of the people dealt with. Inflation is negative and counterproductive. If we believe that we will continue to encounter spiralling costs, the judgment put into our day-to-day business decisions will deteriorate. We will act as though a dollar spent today can always be repaid with cheaper dollars tomorrow. Our values and expectations are distorted proportionately. These pressures, for example, lead labor to demand uneconomical, nonproductive settlements which only help to drive many jobs to more competitive environments.

Managers continue to feel frustrated because there seems to be nothing we can do to impact or slow down the forces of inflation. We know inflation is bad, but we simply don't know how to deal with it on a personal level.

The Status Quo

On a personal level also, we seem to be developing into a nation grown comfortable with the status quo. The United States was once a society built upon change. Now resistance to change predominates. This resistance frustrates the innovative manager who recognizes that change is essential to improvement and competitive success.

The impact of such attitudes was demonstrated in a recent experience. The program permitting direct deposit of Social Security checks into banking and savings institutions had just been announced. In New York, savings and loan associations and savings banks embraced the opportunity immediately. An executive of a large, old-line commercial bank, on the other hand, reacted by stating that his institution really didn't want "those people" as customers. Thus, his resistance to change was effectively shutting his institution out from a multibillion-dollar market that had become available for the asking.

A possible saving grace, if it can be regarded that way, is that this resistance to change seems to be prevalent. In any given industry, most companies will be peopled with the same kind of resisters. The executive who is able to foster an environment which embraces change may enjoy a strong competitive edge.

Process vs. Results

Increasingly, motivated managers are being frustrated on hearing the phrase: "I did my best." The problem is that this is almost always said without any relationship to results, success, or satisfaction. More and more, individuals disclaim ownership of the outcomes or results of their efforts. They are content simply to do their little thing with no concern for quality, then to pass along the work to someone else.

The next person does the same, and so on, with no built-in concern for results or satisfaction. Productivity is measured only as fulfillment of a process which is imbued with a life of its own. Increasingly specialized tasks become increasingly meaningless to the people performing them.

To appreciate the massiveness of this preoccupation with process rather than results, consider what has happened across the country in our education systems. Students have been processed rather than taught. Our laws have mandated attendance rather than performance. People have reacted accordingly. Schools have become caretakers. This has led to widely publicized results where high-school graduates are functionally illiterate.

Results-oriented managers can only be frustrated as they encounter people with treadmill attitudes.

Satisfaction

In the face of such apparent, prevalent dissatisfaction, executives are increasingly frustrated by people who seem to want more for doing less. On responsible consideration, these demands tend to shape up as more apparent than real. People really don't want to do less. They want meaning and satisfaction in the work they are assigned. They seek challenges. When meaning is missing, apathy sets in.

The management need lies in recognizing that work builds people and that challenging work builds good people. Creating an atmosphere where people can derive satisfaction from what they do can contribute directly to enhancing the quality of services rendered and the productivity realized in delivering them.

Growth vs. Stagnation

Perhaps the final frustration faced by many executives comes from the egalitarian attitudes we find all around us. As individuals and as societies, we seem preoccupied with a desire to divide and equalize our resources. Somehow people have gotten the idea that they have vested rights in things that belong to others. This, in turn, destroys or diminishes feelings of responsibility for results of individual efforts.

As people, as organizations, as industries, and even as nations, we seem to have become mired in a preoccupation with how we are going to go about dividing a fixed-sized pie into equal, diminishing-sized slices. This is counterproductive, frustrating. We should be concentrating our energies on ways to increase the size of the pie. The basic challenge lies in stimulating individual attitudes toward growth rather than in concentrating on allocating what we already have. Walter B. Wriston, Chairman of Citicorp, put this need extremely well in the title of a recent address before a dinner of United Nations ambassadors: "Let's Create Wealth – Not Allocate Shortages."

WHAT DO THESE FRUSTRATIONS MEAN?

All of these frustrations are symptomatic. They reflect the emergence of a mature industrial nation which has spawned a society more preoccupied with the allocation of resources than with its continuing economic growth.

One of the key characteristics of our mature industrial society is that we have become a service – rather than an industrialized or manufacturing – economy. This same course has been run by other nations and other societies. Ours is not yet as mature as some. Rather, at this point we could describe ourselves as a society in its first generation of industrial maturity and service emphasis.

Recognizing this first-generation status, we acquire an opportunity to impact the delivery of services which form the bulk of our gross national product so as to avoid following other maturing economies into a seemingly inevitable decline. Just as the United States led the industrial revolution, it may just be possible for us to lead a service revolution as well.

To accomplish this, we must recognize and build upon our strengths. As a society, our major strengths have rested upon our competitive capitalistic instincts. If the transition into a service economy is to succeed, we must figure out a way to take these competitive instincts with us.

What does this mean? It means that we want to avoid a national, regulated policy covering delivery of the increasing amounts of services consumed. We must remain just as competitive in devising and delivering services as we have been in the making and marketing of products. A national-level policy would ignore these highly developed competitive urges.

On the other hand, if we recognize that management policy is our chief means of remaining competitive in an evolving service environment, a climate for growth rather than stagnation can be created. We can generate new wealth rather than slicing existing pies into ever-smaller wedges.

WHAT ARE THE CHARACTERISTICS OF A FIRST-GENERATION SERVICE ECONOMY?

How do we know we have become a service economy? It's readily apparent. The majority of our gross national product now encompasses private and governmental services. Some 60 percent of our work force is now engaged in nonmanufacturing and nonagrarian pursuits.

Private-Sector Conglomeration

In the private portion of our service sector, one of the clear characteristics of enterprises is the ease with which they can be taken over by other, larger organizations. Thus, competition has forced or encouraged a continuing process of acquisition and merger. A trend appears to be developing much as it did earlier in the manufacturing sector. This has led to dominance over the delivery of services by a decreasing number of super-organizations. For proof, consider what has happened in commercial banking, insurance, investment banking, hotels, airlines, and computer-service organizations. To illustrate: probably 80 percent of commercial deposits currently reside in 10 percent of the banks. There are more than 14,000 banks in the United States. But less than 150 money-center institutions dominate the field.

This monolith continues to grow as super-organizations break down and blur traditional industry boundaries. Life insurance companies are writing casualty policies. Casualty companies are underwriting in the life area. Commercial and investment banking are rapidly blending into each other. Investment banking organizations are also absorbing insurance carriers.

Down the road, it is possible to foresee a day when this consolidation trend leaves a handful of financial services super-organizations functioning on a worldwide basis. These opportunities have been widely recognized and acted upon. For example, British-American Tobacco recently acquired Gimbels. Mobil acquired Montgomery Ward. Loews/CNA came together as a consolidation of entertainment, hotel, and insurance properties and went on to become an international services conglomerate. Transamerica started as a real estate operating company spun off by Bank of America and has gone on to become a financial conglomerate with holdings in oil, insurance, entertainment, auto leasing, and airlines.

Public-Sector Bureaucracy

Another characteristic of a first-generation mature society is the proliferation of government at all levels. In considering the management implications of government as a provider of services, two concerns become dominant. One is the creation or assumption of service functions – both new and acquired – by the government. The other centers around the government's role as regulator.

If the government is to become a major deliverer of services, it is inevitable that a series of monoliths will evolve. These superagencies should be subject to the same scrutiny and evaluation standards as those in the private sector. They should face the same challenges of competition and survival.

In the regulatory area, concerns center around the apparent feeling among bureaucrats that the government is qualified to regulate services in areas where it has no demonstrated capabilities. The irresponsibility which can result from such practices needs no elaboration.

ARE INDUSTRIAL SOLUTIONS APPROPRIATE TO SERVICE SITUATIONS?

Conglomeration in the services area appears to be following the same trend as it did in manufacturing. In manufacturing, a primary rationale for bigness was the benefits of mass production and economies of scale. Do the same principles apply in the services area?

Probably not! To be sure, the same approaches have been tried. There have been untold efforts to mechanize service functions for economies of scale. By and large, these have not worked the same way in the services area as they did in manufacturing.

Why is this so? One reason is that the delivery of services remains labor intensive despite efforts at mechanization. Service organizations continue to face payrolls which comprise up to 80 percent of their operating expenses.

Perhaps even more to the point: services are delivered on a one-to-one basis between the provider and the customer. Satisfaction is realized and can only be measured, in many instances, on a transaction-by-transaction basis.

Thus, as organizations grow in the breadth of services offered and in their absolute size, the quality-productivity connection becomes more appropriate as a controlling force than facilities or mechanized equipment. For example, a small restaurant transacting most of its business over the lunch hour functions directly under the supervision of its owner-manager. Quality standards are part of this individual's way of life. As absentee ownership enters the picture, management policy must replace the proprietor's instincts.

The same, in general, is true when a hotel or real estate property is operated by its owner. Pride of ownership remains the driving force as long as the owner is physically present. As scale and scope expand, policy must fill the inevitable void. People with management responsibility need encouragement through management policy so that they think like owners and act like entrepreneurs.

There are a number of points of difference and reasons why service organizations require a different outlook and distinct policies from manufacturing entities. These include:

- The success of service organizations is dependent upon satisfying customer requirements, not upon production of a product. In effect, a service organization is selling its knowledge of customer needs rather than techniques for production. In a service environment, outputs may have to be continuously variable with customer needs and relationships. In manufacturing, emphasis is upon repeatability.

- The services rendered are themselves dependent upon environmental factors external to and beyond the control of manufacturing-type operations management. In a service situation, the customer presents varying demands directly to the provider. The product delivered must be adaptable to on-the-spot demands. Therefore, flexibility to accommodate infinite change at the point of delivery is essential. By contrast, traditional manufacturing approaches to productivity improvement look inward, concentrating upon the product as the end item. Under such a product orientation, similarity and uniformity of results equate to quality. In a service situation, the premium is on variability and flexibility.

- Traditional, functional organization structures borrowed from manufacturing – particularly from process industries – deliver economies of scale when the result is a tangible, physical product. However, when the same techniques are applied to the delivery of a service, requirements for control measures and management skills needed to maintain quality become excessive. Consider, for example, the processing of a money transfer by a commercial bank on behalf of a major corporate client. The process for handling this kind of transaction is well defined and may even be mechanized. But if the bank relied on mechanization alone, the best quality level which could be assured would be some percentage less than total accuracy and reliability. To achieve this less-than-perfect performance, the bank would have had to establish elaborate inspection and quality control procedures. These are inappropriate because the marketplace demands total reliability and perfection in the completion of these transactions. Thus, the persons who deliver the service must also oversee the transactions.

- Measurements of quality incorporated into most functional, production-oriented systems of management are too remote from the customer to be appropriate in service situations. The worker on a production line may be thousands of miles and a half-dozen layers of distribution removed from the end user of a product. In a service situation, delivery is one-on-one. Transactions may be completed across a desk or a service counter. Feedback is immediate and responsiveness is vital. Functional organizations structured for repeatability of product cannot cope with responsiveness demands of service customers.

WHERE DOES THIS LEAD US?

It's no wonder we're frustrated. As a group, American managers have a commitment to action. We want to deal with our problems. But the appropriate actions have not yet become universally apparent.

Neither are we at the advanced-generation stage of our British, French, or Italian counterparts. We are not yet ready to accept a deterioration of quality of services and productivity of people as inevitable. Our frustrations result chiefly because we are in the first generation of a mature, service-dominated economy.

We are still committed to controlling our own destinies. But time may be running out. If we don't do something about the frustrations we are feeling today, American managers a decade or two from now may become immune to these frustrations. They are more likely to develop a British-type "stiff upper lip."

It is tempting, looking across the Atlantic, to say that the problems which have beset mature service economies in Europe result from excessive demands of labor. It is also tempting to cite developments in the United States – such as the predicament of New York City – to say that the same trend is inevitable here. However, such analyses result primarily from misconceptions: the United States does not have a problem of labor demands, we have a problem of an absence of management commitment. This management commitment must hold that the status quo is not an inevitability. There must be a recognition of the need for and a will to change. There must be boldness in the conceptualizing of change.

Government can't solve these managment problems. The only solution is through management policies backed by a commitment to quality and productivity. This is demonstrated in our successes. The challenge lies in learning from these successes how we can avoid seemingly inevitable failures.

If management of an organization can succeed in establishing a quality-productivity connection through policy, many of the frustrations associated with delivery of service and rising costs can be controlled, possibly even eliminated. If a climate in which services are rendered by people with a feeling of proprietorship over client relationships can be created, customer-satisfaction problems will tend to solve themselves. As a parallel development, costs should become controllable as people increase their productivity.

In other words, management policy is a primary ingredient in determining the quality of services rendered, the productivity realized, and ultimate profitability. Sound service-related policies can enhance results. Unsound or inappropriate policies can lead to deterioration. This is demonstrated in a brief case described in the next chapter.

3
THEREFORE...

WHAT HAVE WE ESTABLISHED SO FAR?

So far, we have inferred from observation that a relationship exists between quality and productivity. We have deduced further that quality and productivity stem from management policies which provide the real basis for competition between service enterprises.

We have also established that major problems of quality and productivity exist in the service sector of an economy which has reached a level of first-generation post-industrial maturity.

In examining the problems of a service economy, we have suggested that manufacturing solutions don't offer universal solutions to service industry problems.

WHAT DO THESE LESSONS MEAN?

Based on these inferences, we can conclude that a vital management challenge in the service area lies in identifying those policies which, when implemented, will result in improved quality and productivity.

One of the confirmations of the position that management policy holds the key to competition is the observation that most progress which has led to economic development – both within an industrial and a post-industrial society – has been achieved through management innovation rather than through technological advancement.

To demonstrate that management policy, rather than technology, drives competitive success, consider the case of Henry Ford. Mr. Ford did not invent mass-production technology. He did not invent the assembly line; he merely put it to work. Alfred Sloan made General Motors work through a system of management which has, on its own, become famous. Then there is IBM. Objectively, it must be concluded that IBM was never a technological leader in computers. Its leadership has been through implementation of innovative management policy, particularly in the marketing area.

It follows, then, that organizations compete through management policy rather than through products or services. Therefore, we can't look to technology for the solution to the quality-productivity equation; we must develop managerial solutions.

WHAT SPECIFIC POLICIES ARE NEEDED?

Given that organizations do, in fact, compete through management policy, attention should be focused, next, on just which policy or set of policies will lead concurrently to enhancement of both quality and productivity.

Of course, a management policy which leads to or provides for an integrated system of management is not the only set of policies a service organization requires to be successful. Other policies will exist in such areas as marketing, human resources, financial control, and quality control. The point is that policy should also be established to assure that the quality-productivity connection is made.

Experience has shown that the management policy which makes the quality-productivity connection most directly should focus on relating and combining three specific elements within an integrated system of management:

- Organizational design
- Management control
- Operational control.

In listing three separate elements, it is important to stress that they are a set. They form a framework for achievement. The entire system must all be implemented concurrently. Neglect in any area can diminish or negate results in the others.

The relationships which should exist in the implementation of these elements of management policy are diagrammed in Figure 3-1. This illustration shows a pyramid structure topped by a set of business plans formed by top-level, senior management. Organization plans are shown as a subset of business plans. Management control, in turn, implements business plans and functions within the organization plans. Management control then establishes a kind of surveillance over operating controls which are the day-to-day functions of the company.

Levels of management are also related to these functions. Business plans and organizational plans are the primary responsibility of senior management. Middle management implements management control while operating management is responsible for operational control.

As will be discussed later, this arrangement meets critical requirements that people who are asked to apply controls should be involved in their planning, design, and implementation.

BOUT AN EXAMPLE TO SHOW HOW 'ANY COMPETES THROUGH POLICY?

ne inter-relationships that exist between policies cov- nizational design, management control, and opera- ol, let's look at a case situation based on recent, real xperience.

npany involved is a national retailer operating some t stores. It is privately held, owned by descendants :. During its formative years, the company experi- ive financial success and rapid growth as a loose .. of relatively independent, autonomous regional operations.

Ultimately, its growth and market dominance were challenged by active competition from mass-merchandising chains. Reactively, the company modeled itself along the lines of its mass-merchandising competitors. Merchandising and distribution were centralized functionally in a single, large facility (1,200 people, $10-$12 million in annual budgets) organized along conventional, product lines. The primary objectives for

A FRAMEWORK FOR MANAGEMENT POLICY

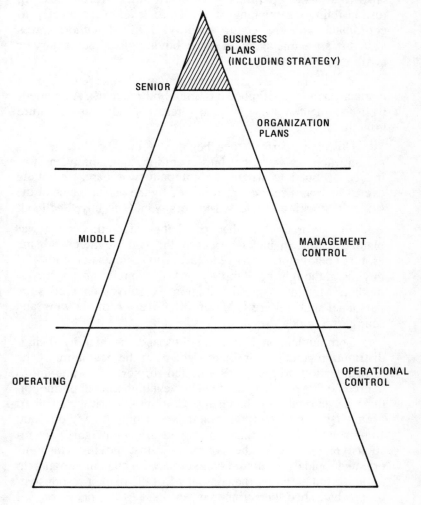

Figure 3-1

this centralization were to realize economies of scale and to gain control over the loose regional organization.

While merchandising and distribution were centralized, store operations remained decentralized in regional and major metropolitan market groupings. Store management responsibilities were primarily operational. Merchandising responsibilities remaining at the store level were chiefly to coordinate with the central facility. Limited authority was vested in store managers for direct buying of supplementary or auxiliary items.

By the time this organization plan was implemented, gross company sales had climbed past the $1 billion mark. A detailed, well-documented strategic plan foresaw steady, strong future growth.

However, performance began sagging shortly after this organization plan was put into operation. Financially, performance declined to where the company was barely breaking even. Quality of service, as reflected by the performance of the stores in stocking articles customers wanted to buy, declined.

Not surprisingly, when problems emerged, change was blamed. Store managers accused the central merchandising group of being unresponsive to local and regional demands – of buying as though the company served a single, homogeneous market. Merchandising-distribution executives charged store personnel with failure to do an effective job of showing and selling the goods they had.

Communication between stores and the merchandising-distribution center, a problem right from the beginning of the reorganization program, deteriorated further. In an attempt to overcome this problem and to achieve a higher level of integration, a National Merchandising Committee was established. Membership included representatives from the regions and some stores. This mechanism proved too cumbersome for responsiveness within the company's fast-moving, fashion-oriented, widely scattered marketplace. Thus, in moving to organize functionally, the company lost the market responsiveness which had been inherent in its earlier, decentralized structure.

This organizational structure and its problems are shown schematically in Figure 3-2. This illustrates that management control was a missing part of this overall organization. Also missing was the middle management responsibility for forming a link between local store operations and overall company management. An attempt to bridge this void was made through committees. However, because committees do not lend themselves to the pinpointing of responsibility, the linkage was never formed effectively.

As one consequence of the management control void, there was no timely feedback to the merchandising center on sales of fashion goods in the regions. Merchandising was planned on a regional basis. But reporting of results was in minute, store-level detail according to merchandise classification.

For all practical purposes, the only management-level reporting consisted of a semiannual, fully absorbed series of profit-and-loss statements. These were detailed by store and department and were not available until three or four months after period closing. Each report consisted of standalone data. There were no comparisons to plan or among regions – or even between periods for the same region. The lack of comparability was highlighted by failure of all of the regions to use the same chart of accounts for financial reporting. Nonetheless, because this was the only information tool available, it was used as a basis for most management decisions, including performance bonuses.

This management control situation contrasted starkly with the presence of strong operating controls. Controls over credit were detailed and tight. Further, the company was a recognized leader in point-of-sale transaction recording and control.

In the face of this deteriorating situation, management remained reluctant to alter the centralized merchandising-distribution organization structure. Over time, the board replaced most members of top management in an effort to improve performance. The new management has moved to recapture the entrepreneurial spirit upon which the company was built.

A study commissioned by the new management revealed that the one region which had consistently produced good results under the centralized merchandising program had apparently done so because its top executive had ignored head-office directives and had run things his own way.

RETAIL DEPARTMENT STORE EXAMPLE

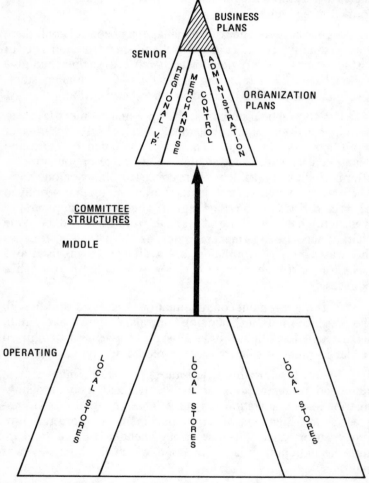

MANAGEMENT
LEVELS

MANAGEMENT
SYSTEM
ELEMENTS

BUSINESS
PLANS

SENIOR

REGIONAL V.P.
MERCHANDISE
CONTROL
ADMINISTRATION

ORGANIZATION
PLANS

COMMITTEE
STRUCTURES

MIDDLE

OPERATING

LOCAL STORES

LOCAL STORES

LOCAL STORES

A MISSING LINK IN THE MANAGEMENT
POLICY FRAMEWORK

Figure 3-2

At this writing, merchandising operations are being decentralized back into the regions. The company is looking for improved quality through the ability to stock its stores to meet local tastes and demands.

Productivity appears on the upswing because regional merchandising personnel, previously limited to a role of coordination with the centralized operation, are now making market-driven buying decisions. Part of the former central staff is being deployed into the regions. Others are being let go. The only major exception is the buying of private-label hard goods, which has remained centralized because this function demands consolidation for volume purchasing.

The company moved to bridge the void in its management and organizational structure through the approach diagrammed in Figure 3-3. As shown, regional organizations were established to form supervisory and communication links between the local stores and top management. These regional organizations cover sales, merchandising, and administrative control.

Further, management controls were implemented. These are represented by notations indicating the presence of departmental profit and loss statements, resources management reports, and productivity reports.

These reports are designed to measure trended profit contribution in a timely, consistent manner, by department, within regions. In addition, measurement and reporting of market share have been implemented. In the future, the same system will encompass manpower control and productivity reporting.

HOW DO YOU GET FROM CASE TO PRACTICE?

Cases are proven, valuable methods for illustrating management principles. However, after studying under the case method, and after being involved in development of many cases in the course of consulting engagements, we have also come to recognize that the case method has its problems. For one thing, there is a temptation to argue with the case itself, looking for more meaning than is really there. Cases, by their nature, are highly simplistic, so much so that active executives tend to find them unrealistic.

It can also be difficult to relate case information back to the theory being presented. When a case is put forward, everybody

RETAIL DEPARTMENT STORE EXAMPLE

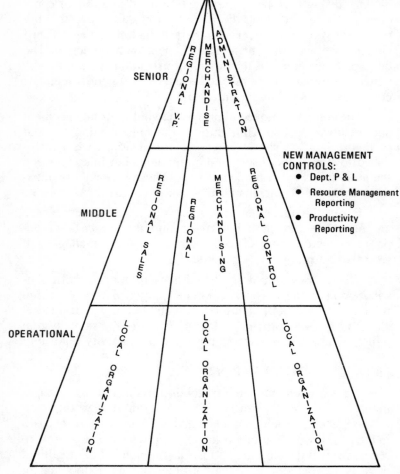

MANAGEMENT LEVELS

MANAGEMENT SYSTEM ELEMENTS

SENIOR

REGIONAL V.P.
MERCHANDISE
ADMINISTRATION

MIDDLE

REGIONAL SALES
REGIONAL
MERCHANDISING
REGIONAL CONTROL

NEW MANAGEMENT CONTROLS:
- Dept. P & L
- Resource Management Reporting
- Productivity Reporting

OPERATIONAL

LOCAL ORGANIZATION
LOCAL ORGANIZATION
LOCAL ORGANIZATION

THE MISSING LINK HAS BEEN REPLACED IN THE MANAGEMENT POLICY FRAMEWORK

Figure 3-3

seems to want to get involved in the specific situation. There is a tendency to lose sight of the theoretical fundamentals being applied – and hopefully learned. Although we believe that theory follows practice in real-world management, it is also true that if a case can't be related to its corresponding theory, the theory itself may have problems. Thus, this book will, in presenting cases, relate them to the management practices they are intended to illustrate.

WHAT DOES THE CASE SHOW?

There was a gap between the strategic plan and the organization expected to implement it. In this case, strategic planning was extremely creative. It was also valid for the nature of the organization. Management knew its customers and the merchandising methods necessary to satisfy its markets. What retailers call "reconceptualization" had been done effectively at the national level. That is, through reconceptualization, management had redefined the stores' merchandising strategy on the basis of identified changes in the marketplace.

The problem lay in plans for implementing this strategy. The people in the field did not identify with or accept responsibility for implementing corporate-level commitments. Regional and local executives could not make the transition between a conceptual plan at the national level and the nuances of implementation to account for regional and local differences. In other words, theoretical concepts could not be translated into practical, real programs by the operating organization. Because the operating organization could not establish this necessary identity, there was no feeling of ownership or commitment in implementing the national-level plans.

Thus, even though strategic plans provide a foundation for management policies which follow, if they are not internalized by the organization, the effect may be disruptive rather than cohesive.

Organizational Design

As in the case of the strategic plan, the organizational design for this company was theoretically and conceptually well done. The design followed a matrix format. The merchandising and store organization were held mutually accountable for results. In theory, the merchandising organization was to formulate plans in close coordination with the store-operations organization. The operating organization would sell the merchandise provided by the centralized support group.

Such sharing of authority and responsibility applies a sophisticated concept generally reserved for high-technology ventures – usually on a project or program basis rather than as a long-range approach to management. In this situation, the focus on the national scope of operations and merchandising overlooked the reality of dramatic differences between marketing regions. The organization was not designed to deal with these inevitable conflicts. In addition, the inherent behavior, or norm, of the management of this organization was not to deal with conflict in a problem-solving manner, but to ignore conflict. Confrontation as a means of conflict resolution was not a normal style by which executives dealt with each other. Yet, the matrix form of organization requires that conflicts be resolved by managers working together in a problem-solving manner. Since the capabilities and reaction times of the people and groups involved were not up to dealing with the problems, a sound organizational theory was misapplied in practice.

Because of this misapplication of organizational principles, extensive management attention and time had to be focused on individual transactions in an effort to deal with responsibilities and accountabilities on a day-to-day basis. Management never did develop a process which could be monitored. Faced with this shortcoming, organizational design did not deal effectively with conflicts which should have been anticipated.

This led to an organizational divisiveness, compounding the conflicts resulting from misunderstanding of strategic plans. Organizational divisiveness, in turn, worsened the adverse relationship between quality and productivity. This happened because the organizational design was not understood at operating levels and because the design itself, including the behavioral aspects of conflict resolution, was probably inappropriate to the problems which had to be solved. In effect, the entrepreneurial spirit required by a merchandising organization was destroyed. Nobody owned the problems anymore.

Management Control

Management controls within this company measured the wrong things. This compounded management's problems. Management controls should monitor performance of the organization in direct comparison with its goals and objectives.

In this instance, there was implied comparability. Management then behaved as if its "numbers" were realistic and reliable. Thus, many management actions were counterproductive, causing good operations to be viewed unfavorably and marginal operations to be rewarded.

In addition, management control reports failed to incorporate measures of performance which were agreed to in advance and related to goals. These should be minimal management control requirements.

Finally, this organization did not make a realistic attempt to distinguish between and gear rewards to differences in performance by managers. In this situation, even a rudimentary system of performance-based rewards would have been better than nothing.

Operational Control

Operational controls were apparently effective in this company. The organization had adequate day-to-day procedures for processing transactions effectively and efficiently.

However, these apparently operated in a vacuum. There was little exception reporting or comparable data which fed into the management control reports. Because of this, the operational controls themselves were not an integral part of the organization. While the controls worked, they did so largely because they had to. The organization simply could not have functioned without operational controls.

WHAT IS THE MANAGEMENT POLICY LESSON?

In the retail organization described, the three elements of management policy – organizational design, management control, and operational control – were not connected. In effect, these elements functioned as three gears in a train, each of which was spinning freely, without being connected to the others. Therefore, these policy elements did not generate the continuity of force necessary to drive the organization toward its goals.

The case thus relates back to the title of this chapter: THEREFORE . . . The point has been made that service organizations compete through a management policy which establishes a quality-productivity connection. If these necessary elements of policy do not function synchronously, as a set, they do not energize the organization competitively.

Why must these three elements of management policy form an integrated set?

If these ingredients of management policy are connected, they form a continuous process. A process can be managed because, by its nature, it is predictable and repeatable. Systems of management can be created for monitoring processes.

The alternative is to attempt to keep track of a series of randomly occurring events. It is far more difficult to monitor and manage unconnected events because there is no way of predicting what decisions will be made, on what day, during which hour, or what they will cover. The loss of predictability leads to a loss of control.

On the other hand, if a process is formalized and communicated to its implementers, the organization, over time, will learn it and apply it as a natural means of accomplishing the enterprise's objectives. The process becomes a way of life. It can be taught and repeated as a system of management. If the implementation of management policy is thought of as a process, it will be less dependent upon individuals and individual styles.

The relationship of the elements of our three-part system within a continuous process is illustrated schematically in Figure 3-4. Dotted-line elements in this diagram indicate that strategic planning and organizational design are periodic processes rather than ongoing operations. Similarly, the feedback from operational control to management control is dictated by exception situations requiring attention, rather than through regular reporting.

HOW DO THE ELEMENTS OF MANAGEMENT POLICY CONNECT TO ACCOMPLISH AN ORGANIZATION'S GOALS AND OBJECTIVES?

In stating that policy generates a process of management, certain characteristics are assumed. A process happens regularly. It

A SYSTEM OF MANAGEMENT

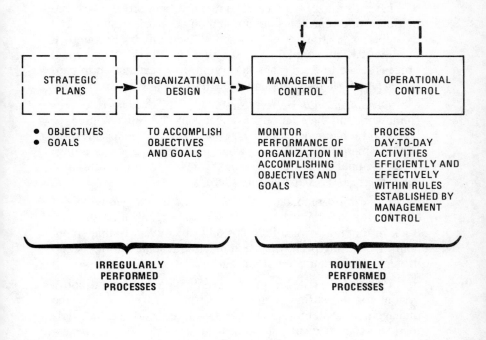

Figure 3-4

is repeated frequently and, in turn, is repeatable. A management process must maintain links with the overall goals and objectives of the organization. These overall goals and objectives encompass a strategic plan.

It is assumed that an organization with a management process handles its strategic planning requirements as needs and opportunities arise. The organization may or may not have a set of formal procedures for strategic planning. However, strategic planning, if it is done effectively, is often opportunity driven rather than time-scheduled. Whatever process is applied is used when and as events or opportunities dictate rather than in response to schedules. This is not to say that strategic planning is only reactive. The word, planning, embodies the feeling of being out in front of events and being sensitive to changes in the external environment that may provide future opportunities.

At any given time, any effectively managed organization will have a strategy in place. The management process covered in this work represents an implementation of strategy. The existence of a strategy is assumed. Given this background, it becomes easier to explain how the elements of our management process relate to each other in driving the organization toward achievement of its goals and objectives.

Organizational design establishes the human-resources framework and the relationships necessary to bring resources to bear upon achievement of goals, objectives, and plans. Presuming that management knows where the organization is going, organizational design establishes the responsibilities and allocates the resources for getting there.

Once the organizational framework exists, *management control* provides the vehicle to be sure the organization stays on track in moving toward its goals and objectives. Management controls measure performance in meeting responsibilities set up through the organizational structure.

Given the existence of an organizational structure and a system for measuring performance, the third element of the management system assures that the organization operates effectively and efficiently in processing its day-to-day (if necessary, minute-to-minute) transactions. The *operational controls* of an organization function within the rules established by its management controls and the relationships within its organizational design.

4
COMMITMENT: A PREREQUISITE FOR IMPLEMENTING CHANGES

IF SERVICE ENTERPRISES COMPETE THROUGH POLICY, WHY AREN'T THEY ALL SUCCESSFUL?

It takes more than policy to create a winning competitor. Policy is passive. Winning demands activity. If policy were all that were needed, service enterprises could copy each other and they would all be successful. Obviously, then, another ingredient is needed to bridge the gap between a winning policy and an actual victory. For a service enterprise, this added ingredient is the commitment of its people.

Putting it another way, good ideas and innovative techniques are valuable starting points. But good ideas are also highly perishable and easily copied. It takes more than good ideas and innovative techniques to build a successful service enterprise. If this were not true, all that businesses would have to do would be to line up and compete for the best brains coming out of business schools each year. The successfully bidding businesses could then think their way to victory.

This isn't how the real world works – at least not for long. Ideas must be translated into actions. These actions, in turn, must be driven by feelings of personal involvement with the directions and aspirations of the organization. Implementers must understand policies. They must feel committed to them. They must have that necessary sense of entrepreneurship which makes them want to succeed.

This need is easily illustrated by pointing to a prevailing failure: the difficulty experienced by governmental organizations at all levels in delivering services effectively and efficiently. Most of us are convinced that government doesn't work the way it should. Why? Part of the answer, we submit, lies in failure to form a bridge, through commitment, between the setting of policies and the delivery of services.

In government, policy making and implementation are separate, distinct, largely unconnected functions. Policies are set by legislators who generate little or no follow-through interest or mechanisms. Implementation is by bureaucrats who, for the most part, have not been consulted about feasibility or workability of newly adopted policies. It is highly improbable that the bureaucrats who implement policy set by legislators will identify with, or feel committed to, the success of resulting programs. Legislators, on the other hand, may well adopt policies which are unworkable because they have not thought through the implementation consequences of their actions. Inefficiencies and ineffectiveness are predictable.

We feel the impact of commitment upon successful implementation of management policies is well described in this excerpt from the writing of W.H. Murray: "... until one is committed there is hesitancy, the chance to draw back, always ineffectiveness. Concerning all acts of initiative (and creation), there is one elementary truth, the ignorance of which kills countless ideas and splendid plans: that the moment one definitely commits oneself, then providence moves too."

HOW DOES COMMITMENT CONTRIBUTE TO SUCCESS?

Committed people are motivated. They care. Commitment goes hand-in-hand with pride.

Considered in the framework of the quality-productivity connection, these traits help contribute to results. Committed people don't need to be directed in what to do on their jobs. As part of their commitment, they will figure out what is needed to produce satisfaction among customers and within their organizations, then do it on their own. Committed people don't have to be inspected to assure the quality of their performance. Quality is implicit in the attitudes of committed people.

When people are committed, they are productive. Their management has made the quality-productivity connection.

HOW DOES IT FEEL TO BE COMMITTED?

Commitment is a personal feeling, a state of mind. It is an internalized involvement by an individual with what has to be done. Commitments are directed toward achievement. People become committed because they are doing something they want to do – as opposed to something they have been told to do.

This is basic to human nature. We generally find time for the things we want to do. We find it difficult to allocate time to accomplish the things that really don't interest us.

As managers, we can't order people to be committed. We can't legislate commitment. We can't dictate it. We can only create an environment where commitment occurs spontaneously.

A feeling of commitment is a feeling that something worthwhile is going on. The committed person can visualize outcomes and can watch them take place. There is excitement and stimulation over a proprietary feeling that the successful results belong to the implementers.

The feeling of commitment is also fragile. It can be shattered by insensitive policies or unforeseen events. Thus, the spirit and feeling of commitment must be monitored, renewed, nurtured continuously.

This is not to suggest that commitment is something hard to attain. Quite to the contrary, the basic forces of human nature favor the establishing of committed attitudes. People want to feel committed. When they are committed to something, they feel good about themselves.

Though there is a natural disposition toward commitment, there are also many acquired defense mechanisms to overcome. In an organizationally oriented society, people tend to develop cynical, negative attitudes which counter the normal tendency to strive for achievement. These defense mechanisms must be dealt with and overcome. However, commitment is achievable because it is a basic, natural, human desire. Commitment is worth striving for because it is so important to success.

HOW IS COMMITMENT RELATED
TO MANAGEMENT POLICY?

Without an environment which encourages and rewards commitment, it doesn't happen. The stimuli must come from management policy.

Commitment can be built through implemented, communicated policies which encourage and reward initiative and responsibility. It is possible to establish policies which encourage people to express their commitments through concern for quality and extra effort when it is called for. It is possible also to establish policies which build sensitivity in managers so that commitment is recognized. On recognition, individuals involved should be commended and rewarded.

Commitment, in short, starts with the framing of policies which encourage people to act as though they are concerned for and involved in the success of their organization. Implementation of such policies should incorporate mechanisms for recognition and encouragement.

Management policy, in short, is both an essential for and a stimulator of commitment.

WHY IS COMMITMENT SO IMPORTANT?

A committed organization can make a marginal idea work well. On the other hand, an uncommitted organization can destroy even a superb idea.

This phenomenon is encountered every day. We have all met customer-contact personnel – bank tellers, retail clerks, waiters – who extend themselves for customer satisfaction. We appreciate their commitment, particularly when we experience the opposite extreme in the form of persons who are "doing their job and no more." On receiving services from committed people, we, the customers, feel important. Satisfaction is high.

While satisfaction is easy to identify and explain on an individual level, it is difficult to find examples of how corporate policies have molded attitudes and achieved commitment. This is possibly because we are conditioned to think of organizations as impersonal and find it hard to make the connection between personal experiences and management policies. However challenging, it is possible for companies to adopt and implement policies which attain commitment of the entire organization. All individual members of an organization are able to internalize and associate with such policies.

For an example, consider the positive attitudes which pervade the organization of Sears Roebuck and Co. From headquarters, to regional management, to store management, to the people on the sales floors, everyone behaves as though he or she is personally committed to what the organization stands for. The vast majority of transactions with customers in a wide variety of environments are positively perceived and satisfactorily executed. Individual employees feel that the success of the organization is up to them, that they are making a contribution. There is no leaving of service concerns to someone else.

Perhaps this is best illustrated in the handling of returns and adjustments throughout the Sears organization. In all of retailing, such transactions hold the greatest potential for negative results – for aggravation on the part of the salespeople and frustration on the part of customers. However, Sears has adopted and implemented policies which create situations in which customers and salespersons are not adversaries. Returns or adjustments are perceived and implemented as positive opportunities to prove the service orientation of the organization as a whole. The customer is not asked to behave as though he or she were trying a case, with the salesperson sitting as a judge. The entire transaction is entered into with the salesperson committed to build upon existing levels of customer satisfaction. Potentially negative situations are turned, almost invariably, into positive experiences.

To illustrate how opposite results can develop, consider the case of the 70-store chain cited earlier. This organization went into a decline largely because personnel in the stores lost their commitment. They had no sense of ownership over the ideas or merchandising programs they were asked to implement. They had no role in the process of selecting merchandise and delivering services. They had lost the mechanisms for achieving customer satisfaction. Their attitudes reflected a lack of constructive management policy and a management failure to create an environment promoting commitment. It isn't a question of whether the management policies were good or bad. The point is that the organization didn't feel proprietorship over the policies and programs. Lack of commitment generated a deterioration in the quality of service.

In general, then, commitment breeds good service while a lack of commitment leads to a deterioration of service. It is, therefore, desirable to have commitment throughout a service organization. A real challenge lies in achieving a top-to-bottom commitment.

HOW IS COMMITMENT ACHIEVED?

Commitment is built by transferring the ownership of good ideas. This may be a presumptuous statement. But the logic is straightforward: people are more readily committed to conclusions they have reached on their own than they are to ideas or instructions presented by others. People work harder to achieve plans they have set for themselves than they do for those which may have been prepackaged for them.

We have observed a variety of styles and techniques through which managers attempt to transfer ownership of ideas – which equates to securing commitment for their implementation.

Probably the most laborious – and possibly the most effective – technique has been applied within a number of Japanese organizations we have observed. Japanese managers seem willing to invest tremendous amounts of time to evolve consensus for new ideas. Consensus, in turn, leads to a high mutual commitment. The process is deliberate, time consuming, thoughtful, and thorough. Once it has been completed, we have seen achievement of change accomplished in what would be record time by United States standards. Under what we perceive to be the Japanese style of management, no announcement of objectives is permitted until a thorough commitment has been achieved and attainment is virtually certain.

Other management styles or techniques seek transference of ownership through a variety of approaches to conflict resolution. Some organizational cultures or behavioral norms attempt to resolve conflicts and attain commitment by avoiding direct confrontation over current or potential problems. This doesn't really result in a transfer of ownership or a commitment to a course of action because it assures a maintenance of the *status quo*. Bureaucratic organizations are often characterized by this type of non-resolution. By avoiding or smoothing over conflicts, such organizations effectively prevent a feeling or transference of ownership in new ideas. Thus, all that can be accomplished is to perpetuate existing attitudes and practices. This was the case in the example cited in the preceding chapter. Management difficulties arose in the department store chain partly due to absence of a problem-solving behavioral norm as a means of resolving inevitable conflicts brought about through the matrix organization.

Another observed form of conflict resolution utilizes a forcing or bargaining style. Conflict resolution is treated as a negotiation or a political compromise. The forcing and bargaining norm may result in transference of ownership, and also a commitment, if the sponsor of a new idea or program is so strong that the others have no choice but to agree and follow, perhaps out of fear. This gets the job done in the short range. However, we believe there is room to question how lasting a commitment can be achieved and how effective participation will be if individuals do not identify with the idea or program.

The most effective means of conflict resolution and resulting transference of ownership and commitment we have seen calls for participation by people who will be asked to implement new ideas or programs. This approach promotes confrontation and problem solving as a way of life. Ownership of good ideas is transferred to all members of the group because they participate actively in resolving conflicts, solving problems, and developing the programs ultimately implemented. In this way, people acquire both intellectual involvement and intuitive commitment because they have taken an active part in shaping the idea. A true feeling and spirit of ownership results.

This confrontation and problem-solving norm for conflict resolution is, in itself, a management process. As such, it requires a great deal of leadership skill and practice.

A challenge, then, lies in stimulating members of an organization to think constructively about their common problems and goals. If these individuals come to their own conclusions, they don't have to be told what to do or the way it should be done. If they believe in an idea, they will implement it enthusiastically and constructively.

One essential for transferring ownership lies in transferring credit as well. Management doesn't have to own all of the good ideas in an organization. The people who are implementing the ideas should be able to identify with them, to gain a sense of fulfillment. This can be an extremely difficult concept to grasp and implement. There is a natural tendency to take credit for innovation and success. Sharing success is an acquired but constructive habit.

Another necessary realization is that the feeling of commitment throughout the organization must be renewed continuously. There are no permanent, or even periodic, commitments. A person doesn't come to work and say: "I feel committed for today." Rather, commitment must be demonstrated and renewed with every transaction or event in which each individual participates. There is no selective commitment. Commitment must be total, consistent, and continuous. It must be demonstrated in the face of difficulty as well as when things are going well.

Achievement of commitment requires a management style which provides for conflict resolution and problem solving while also promoting teamwork and fostering individual maturity. As indicated, it involves putting down the tendency to own good ideas. The manager seeking commitment of teammates does not think, feel, or act in terms of "I." Success-oriented thinking is in terms of "we" and "us." Success should belong to everyone who participates in achieving it. The organization should provide an environment which promotes the necessary participation.

To illustrate, consider the team management policies implemented at Citibank. Management analyzed its markets and their requirements, then created what are, in effect, a set of "minibanks" to serve them. Corporate planning for the "minibanks" was minimal. Commitment was achieved by permitting managers to whom responsibility for individual "minibanks" was delegated to determine what services were to be offered and to plan for their delivery. Individual managers were held accountable and responsible for their own actions. The managers were thus committed in a way and to an extent which never could have been achieved if they had been told what to do. (The plan of organization and customer relationships of the "minibanks" are described in Chapter 6.)

Another prerequisite for commitment is top-level support. Commitment is enhanced through leadership examples. This is well illustrated in this excerpt from an address by Edward B. Rust, President of State Farm Insurance Companies:

"I was in an office conference the other day in Bloomington, Illinois, when a customer of ours in Houston got me on the telephone. He had a problem that I was able to help him with. When our telephone conversation concluded, one of the people in my office commented that an efficiency expert would be appalled that I would interrupt an important meeting to involve myself in the problems of one of our 20 million policyholders. It would strike him as an inefficient use of executive time. My response was – and I deeply believe this – that the day I refuse calls from customers is the day I should resign as head of the companies, because that is the day I will have begun to lose contact with the real world in which we operate.

"Share this little fantasy with me:

"Suppose every American product had a sticker on it, right up there where everyone could see it – smack in the middle of a car's dashboard, right on the side of the toaster, or in big letters by the dial of the TV set, and it read:

" 'If this thing doesn't work like we said it would, call our president,' followed by his name and telephone number.

"It's hard to imagine the impact this would have, but I can tell you a couple of things that would happen. Those consumer complaint statistics that come up in orderly columns from the computers would suddenly come very much alive, bristling with humanity, and in a very short span of time the corporation president would acquire a very sure sense of reality – as well as an unlisted phone number.

"You see, my name is on about 20 million insurance policies. If our service to our insured breaks down – as it sometimes does – or if misunderstandings arise that aren't cleared up elsewhere in the organization, the policyholder will sometimes look at the bottom line of the last page of his insurance contract, see my name and call me. And if he doesn't get me, he gets one of my assistants.

"Quite often, he is irate and frustrated and has carefully marshalled the arguments he is sure he will need. But when I listen to his complaint, and if it's clear to me that he has not received what he has a right to expect from us, I apologize to our customer and tell him what I'm going to do to get things back on track for him. At that point, there is often stunned silence on the customer's end of the phone line, and I sometimes have to say 'hello' two or three times to awaken him from shock.

"Why should candor and a desire to correct errors be such a startling experience for an American consumer to encounter in American business?

"I have been told that these observations may make of me something of a pariah in the American business community, but I'll take that risk because I have great faith in the reason and good sense of most business leaders and managers."

The J.C. Penney Company grew from one store to more than 1,200 partly by following policies which demand and reward commitment. Each store manager is encouraged through direct impact on earnings and professional growth to act as though he is in business for himself. It is the responsibility of each store manager to know the local market well enough to tailor inventories and service policies to customer demands. Managers have broad authority and responsibility to produce results through their own effort and innovation. The record keeping system of the corporation is designed to measure and report on performance at the individual unit level. Emphasis is on support for the store manager, who accepts and affirms performance goals for the individual unit and then relies on the resources of the company to help meet them.

The State Farm example illustrates top-level commitment. The policies at J.C. Penney demonstrate the kind of management policies which promote commitment at operating levels. Both illustrate how commitment builds responsive service and that commitment at all levels contributes to an organization's success.

HOW DO YOU KNOW WHEN
YOU DON'T HAVE COMMITMENT?

The most telling symptom of an uncommitted organization lies in the amount of time it takes for change to occur. One of the biggest reasons that it takes so long for governmental agencies to implement change, for example, is the pervading lack of commitment; there is no feeling of ownership on the part of the people responsible for implementing the change. On the other hand, in a committed organization characterized by adaptiveness and marketing flexibility, people don't have to be sold on change. Once they understand what is needed, they go ahead.

Any manager who has ever competed with a committed organization knows that this can be a frightening, awesome experience. Consider, for example, the success of Western International Hotels in developing and operating a succession of new properties. Success results largely because the manager of each individual facility has the latitude and resources necessary to adapt service to the needs of individual markets. Similarly, consider what it must be like to manage a retail outlet and learn that a Bloomingdale's or a Sears is moving into the neighborhood. In the case of Bloomingdale's, competition takes the form of a flexible, dynamic organization committed to success through delivery of services, rather than the displaying and selling of merchandise. In the case of Sears, it has been said that they don't buy a market, they serve it.

HOW DOES ALL THIS LEAD TO
IMPLEMENTATION OF POLICIES?

Once achieved and made a part of the organization, commitment generates an environment for implementation of management policies. The setting of policy itself is, as discussed above, relatively easy. Establishing systems to monitor and report on operations is not especially difficult. This is because people throughout an organization tend to understand operating systems which are essential to doing business.

Establishing management control over the carrying out of policies is much more difficult. This is because policy implementation deals with elements of how people feel and think about themselves, about the directions of their organization, and how they react to events they encounter. When people are committed, they care about the way their business is running. They implement management controls because they believe in them.

Implementation is a matter of management fundamentals, analogous to the fundamentals of blocking, tackling, and endurance to which winning football teams dedicate themselves. To illustrate this point, consider the success which has been enjoyed by McDonald's. McDonald's does not sell hamburgers. They sell quality service, healthfulness, cleanliness, and a secure, comfortable place for a family to visit. It was relatively easy to incorporate this into the advertising slogan: ''We do it all for you.'' It was more difficult, and far more important in the long run, to ingrain the commitment and the activities to implement the commitment throughout the organization, down to the level of the people who clean the tables and sweep the parking lots. Implementing this policy of quality has led to clear-cut championship performance, as evidenced by the market domination which has resulted.

The methods through which management attains an organizational commitment to new ideas and change become vital ingredients in achieving the quality-productivity connection. When an organization enthusiastically embraces a direction which focuses on quality and productivity, that organization is committed.

5
THE SOLUTION: A SYSTEM OF MANAGEMENT

HOW ABOUT REVIEWING THE PROBLEM WE ARE GOING TO SOLVE?

By inference, we have established that service enterprises compete on the basis of how well they have formed and implemented management policies. The rationale has been extended to indicate that the same set of policies can be applied to enhance both the quality of services delivered and the productivity realized. In effect, quality and productivity are regarded as equal sides of an equation. Quality is measured in terms of level of customer satisfaction. Productivity represents the results realized from resources, including human effort.

It is generally accepted in management circles that problems associated with quality of services and productivity call for management solutions rather than technological innovation. Most pronouncements in this area stop at about this point. That is, there is general agreement that these are management problems. But there is very little said about how these problems are approached and solved.

We submit that the solution lies in a system of management encompassing three elements which, when implemented as a unit or set, form a continuous process for the achievement of outcomes in which quality and productivity are directly related and equated. These three elements are organizational design, management control, and operational control.

WHAT DO WE MEAN BY ORGANIZATIONAL DESIGN?

Marvin Bower of McKinsey & Co., in his book, *The Will to Manage,* defines organizational design as a process for the development of a plan of organization which provides "the harness that helps people pull together in performing activities in accordance with strategy, philosophy, and policies."

This simple definition, we believe, is far easier to understand and internalize than others we have seen which are perhaps more precise technically. Textbook definitions of organizational design tend to be stated in terms of responsibilities, accountabilities, authority, and other terms which delineate actions which may be taken.

In Mr. Bower's definition, we feel the key words are: *people, harness, pull,* and *together.* These terms imply that an organization consists of people who are loosely held together, who are going in the same direction because they choose to rather than because they are driven.

The term *organizational structure* serves, in itself, to define some of the inherent problems. *Structure* implies rigidity, crispness, precision, balance, and fixed boundaries. These characteristics really oppose the natural inclinations and aspirations of people. Real organizations are seldom tightly defined, balanced, or cast in fixed roles.

The beauty of Mr. Bower's definition, therefore, is that it produces a word picture which connotes movement, freedom, and purpose. We believe an organization should be thought of as free-flowing in nature and that organizational design should permit the implementation of plans which achieve this end.

What is the Role of Organizational Design?

The purpose of an organizational design is to contribute to achievement of overall strategic plans. The goals and objectives of the strategic plans should thus drive the organizational design effort. For a service enterprise, these goals and objectives should be geared, among other things, toward attaining quality and productivity. The design of the organization should be developed with these objectives in mind.

Willing these objectives into being through policy statements alone won't make them happen. It is necessary, rather, to look at the outcomes an organization will be asked to produce. The question can be asked: what results will be produced by having people work together that way?

To illustrate, it is possible to organize an insurance operation for flexibility of service in delivering low-cost products to broad, general markets. However, if the strategy of the organization is to seek out and serve a narrow, homogeneous marketplace with specialized products, the breadth and flexibility which may be built in are, in effect, wasted.

The role of organizational design, then, is to assure a matching of the organization with its mission. (The organizational design element of our management process is covered in Chapters 6 and 7.)

WHAT DO WE MEAN BY MANAGEMENT CONTROL?

Professor Robert N. Anthony of the Harvard Business School defines management control as a process by which managers assure that resources are used effectively and efficiently in accomplishing the organization's objectives.

The key words in this definition are: *process, managers, resources, efficiently,* and *effectively.* These words, to us, communicate the idea that management control establishes a continuous process which links related activities. Management control is a *process* performed by *managers.* Its existence implies the allocation and management of *resources.* The term *effectively* implies that the resources are used in the right places, while the term *efficiently* implies that the results are realized economically.

Overall, management controls within an organization are directed toward realizing its strategies and objectives.

What is the Role of Management Control?

Management controls are closely related to the organizational design established for an enterprise. Both are tied, in turn, to implementing strategies and meeting objectives. Where organizational design provides the harness that helps people pull together, management control provides assurance that, in fact, those objectives are being met.

The value of management controls can be illustrated by

citing the situation of a major money-center bank. This institution designed elements of its organization specifically to provide quality service in handling money transfers for corporate clients. In implementing the organizational design, however, no mechanism was created to monitor the performance of services and to provide assurances that quality standards, as perceived by clients, were being met. This oversight resulted in a situation where management was unaware that some of its major corporate clients were dissatisfied with the quality of money-transfer services.

The role of management control, then, lies in monitoring organizational performance and providing feedback when and as management's attention is required. (This element of our system of management is discussed in Chapter 8.)

WHAT DO WE MEAN BY OPERATIONAL CONTROL?

For a service organization, operational control encompasses both process and product. The words, *process* and *product*, indicate that operational control is both a method by which the day-to-day functions of the organization are carried out and also constitutes the actual service rendered to customers.

The integration of process and product is a major uniqueness of service entities. This integration also contributes to the relationship between quality and productivity – since both end results stem from a single process, the procedures for their realization are inter-related.

What is the Role of Operational Control?

Operational control, in effect, encompasses the systems and procedures which execute and deliver the results called for in management controls. These are the actual services to customers. Operational controls, in turn, are implemented by people working in the relationships established in organizational design.

To illustrate, demand deposit accounting is both a product or service and an operational control within a commercial bank. It is a service which enables customers to write checks against their accounts in the bank. It is a control covering the execution of procedures for properly entering, recording, and reporting on the status of customer accounts.

Demand deposit accounting also represents execution of an organizational design encompassing responsibilities for service to a specific market segment. The same system also uses resources and produces results which should be specified within management controls.

(Operational controls are covered in Chapter 9.)

WHERE DOES THIS SYSTEM OF MANAGEMENT LEAD?

This integrated approach to management should lead to solution of the quality-productivity equation through techniques of management innovation rather than through the application of technology.

The term *management innovation* implies that there are no new techniques or methods involved. Management innovation is achieved by incorporating existing tools and techniques into a set, or continuity, which can be applied consistently. This is what management innovation is all about – adapting and combining existing tools which, though not unique individually, provide a breakthrough collectively. Individually, no one technique utilized will solve the equation. Collectively, they do produce workable answers.

6
DESIGNING THE RESPONSIVE ORGANIZATION

WHY DO WE CALL ORGANIZATIONAL DESIGN A PROCESS?

Our definition, in the last chapter, described organizational design as a process which provides "the harness that helps people pull together..." to develop a plan of organization which meets overall strategies, goals, and objectives.

In saying that organizational design is a process, we identify it as a series of actions which, when completed, delivers a specified end result. For organizational design, that specified result is a plan of organization which should be thought of as a dynamic, living element of management policy rather than as a static structure represented by a chart composed of lines and symbols.

As a dynamic element of management policy, organizational design deals with constantly changing and emerging goals and objectives. These are refined continuously as an organization matures and its managers sharpen their perspectives and shape new policies.

The specific insight which we believe is significant in competing through organizational design is that a business must be organized to reflect two elements of policy:

1. The desired outcomes of the business, usually defined in terms of objectives and goals

2.   The basic beliefs and policies integral to the culture of the business.

It is important that these desired outcomes and culture of the business be utilized as a framework for organizational design. Without this guidance, it is possible for an organization to produce results other than those targeted by management. Every organization will produce outcomes. The real management challenge lies in making sure that the ones realized are those which management wants. Management beliefs and desires for outcomes are, of course, subject to change or adjustment as a result of accumulated experience or maturity. As such changes in culture or desired results occur, organizational designs should be altered or adapted to reflect them.

WHAT IS THE MANAGEMENT SIGNIFICANCE OF ORGANIZATIONAL DESIGN?

Organizational design is critically important to a service organization because it allocates and guides the efforts of people. People, in turn, are the main resource of any service enterprise, accounting for up to 80 percent of operating costs.

Further, organizational design, if implemented correctly, can be achieved in less time than other management changes, such as development of facilities or systems. However, to realize results from organizational design, the people involved must be sensitive to and cognizant of the projected outcomes and basic beliefs cited earlier. These projected outcomes should include both the elements of the quality-productivity connection for the specific organization and the basic beliefs and culture which influence the behavior of individuals within the organization. Given the presence of these conditions, organizational design is the place where management can realize greater results in improving quality of performance and productivity – and do so in less time – than through any other approach.

Thus, if management wishes to improve quality and productivity to make people more responsive to customer needs, organizational relationships are the places to initiate changes. These should precede changes to either management controls or operational controls.

Quality and productivity are much more sensitive to organizational relationships than to controls which might be built into the procedures. Management leverage achievable through organizational changes which focus on quality and productivity is potentially enormous. This ability to achieve outcomes through organizational design clearly demonstrates the principle that service enterprises compete and realize success through management innovation, not through technological innovation. *Management innovation is prerequisite to application of technological innovation.*

Because the time required for implementation of organizational design is much shorter than for other elements of management policy, people can quickly perceive results of organizational design programs. A feeling of success is generated more quickly through organizational design than through any other element of policy. A will to win is reinforced by successful completion of an organizational change. Results are realized far more quickly than through implementation of technical processes which may or may not be successful, but are likely to be frustrating.

Quality and productivity are people and organizational issues in service enterprises. Therefore, management profits by putting high priority on changes in this area – changes which can be implemented quickly, effectively, and efficiently.

HOW DO COMPANIES COMPETE THROUGH ORGANIZATIONAL DESIGN?

We have established that service enterprises compete primarily through policy and that organizational design is the first and largest element of management policy affecting an enterprise's competitive stance. It is also true, therefore, that companies compete through their organizational designs.

This is true for service enterprises because of both their labor intensity and the uniqueness of each individual transaction. Each service rendered must be identified as acceptable to a particular customer. Therefore, flexibility and judgment must be present at the point where the transaction takes place.

In talking about people's sensitivity to the delivery of services, Peter Drucker uses the term "knowledge worker." This phrase recognizes the fact that more than half of all employed workers in the United States are in the service sector. Generally, service workers are middle-class persons who represent the better educated portion of the population. Achieving quality and productivity in the delivery of services is entirely dependent upon the manner in which these people work together and organize themselves to perform in a service environment where all transactions are unique and individual. Workers organize their activities and divide the tasks to be handled among themselves to achieve quality and productivity on a current, dynamic basis.

The principles applied to organizing and developing workers have changed markedly as we have moved into a service economy. Today, a productive knowledge worker, according to Drucker, needs to be led rather than managed, directed rather than controlled. Drucker argues that service organizations do not lend themselves to fixed procedures for worker performance. There is no one best way in which knowledge work can be performed.

This is in sharp contrast with the conventional, functional design of organizations pioneered by large manufacturing enterprises and copied widely by many service entities. Within a functional organization, like activities are grouped together, as illustrated in Figure 6-1. Typical breakdowns include marketing, finance, sales, production, engineering, and so on.

When the country was still undergoing the industrial revolution, Frederick W. Taylor contributed a major breakthrough by developing the principle for subdividing tasks to achieve consistency in mass production. These principles may have made a major contribution in factories 50 years ago, but, in a service environment, the management challenge no longer lies in breaking down tasks. Success results from how well people work together. Under such conditions, it stands to reason that the enterprise which is best organized will be the most competitive.

A functional organization works well as long as outcomes can be defined in terms of repeatability and similarity of results. Where the outcome is an individually rendered service, organizational design must be planned to assure high levels of quality and productivity. These are minimal, mandatory objectives around which service enterprises should be organized. There may, of course, be other organizational objectives. But these two – quality and productivity – should be incorporated in

SIMPLIFIED EXAMPLE OF A CLASSIC — FUNCTIONAL ORGANIZATIONAL DESIGN

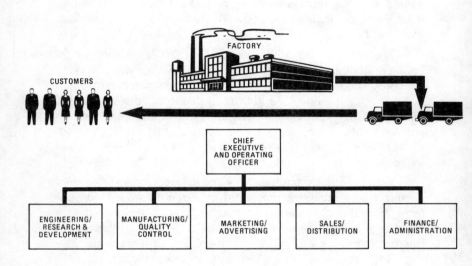

**10,000 PEOPLE
SIMILAR TASKS**

Figure 6-1

projected outcomes for all service enterprises. An organizational plan designed to respond to market situations is illustrated in Figure 6-2. In effect, this organizational structure inverts the conventional organization chart. The customer is at the top, served by teams organized around customer segments or characteristics. Each team is self-contained, with access to virtually all of the resources necessary to serve its customers.

SIMPLIFIED EXAMPLE OF AN ORGANIZATIONAL DESIGN FOR A MARKET ENVIRONMENT

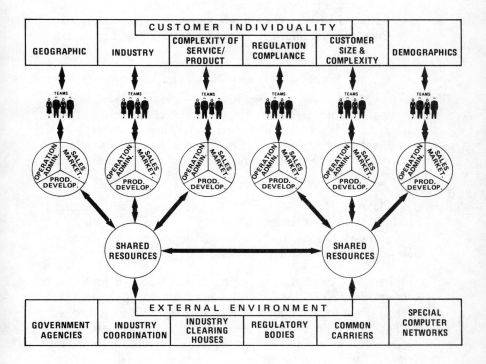

Figure 6-2

HOW ABOUT SOME EXAMPLES?

Among the world-class service organizations which stand out for their competitive successes is K mart. Organizational design is one of the elements of competitive policy to which K mart owes its success. This was confirmed in an article (July, 1977) in *Fortune* magazine that attributed much of K mart's success to policies established by its former president, Harry Cunningham. As part of the decision to get into discounting in the early sixties, Cunningham described a one-day study of the operations of an innovative discounter, E.J. Korvette. Among other areas of interest, he studied the methods and policies of Eugene Ferkhauf, founder of Korvette. Cunningham was quoted as saying:

> "Ferkhauf was just a hell of a merchant . . . But he was running the whole show single-handedly. The concept was great. He just didn't have the organization to implement it."

The article then says about Cunningham:

> "His genius lay in organization – giving store managers considerable leeway within strict centralized precepts for size and layout of the stores, and to a great extent, the merchandising. He soon developed a well-oiled machine that has been cranking out K marts with cookie-cutter precision ever since."

Clearly, Harry Cunningham competed with Eugene Ferkhauf through management policy – specifically through organizational design. There is no question about this. There is also no question about the results.

Part of Cunningham's design concept was to build the K mart organization for flexibility and market responsiveness. In the *Fortune* article another K mart executive is quoted as saying: "We'll never be a fashion leader . . . but we will be the fastest follower there ever was." As a statement of company strategy, this is clearcut and understandable. This desired outcome was reflected in K mart's organizational design. The *Fortune* article comments:

> "The accent in the talk about retail diversification is on doing the job internally rather than by acquisition. Company executives believe their own people will be best able to deal with the complexities of developing new niches for specialty ventures and melding them into the corporation without impinging on K marts. Top managers cite several instances in which they have moved people into new areas with great success – e.g., the former hardware buyer who established K mart Enterprises, the automotive and sporting-goods subsidiary.

"K mart works hard to develop that kind of flexibility as well as the gung-ho spirit that is almost palpable throughout the organization..."

The same executive is then quoted as saying: "What makes the whole thing work... is people – training, loyalty, dedication, and pride – and the delegation of authority."

Organizational design is also a critical factor in the domination which McDonald's has achieved in the fast-food field. Management policies at McDonald's call for a continuing series of quality inspections of all outlets. Results of these inspections affect the awarding of future franchises to existing operators. These elements of McDonald's operations were described in a *Business Week* (July 11, 1977) article:

"... McDonald's money machine is used to finance the industry's tightest corporate scrutiny of store operations. At the core of that effort are the company's 190 field consultants who each year make two three-day inspections of each McDonald's store, grading operators on the quality of their products, speed, friendliness of service, and cleanliness. At the end of each inspection, the operator is handed a 17-page report evaluating his operations with suggestions for improvements to boost sales volume.

"Normally the incentive for more volume is enough to encourage an operator to improve, but the grading system is also used to determine whether McDonald's will grant the franchisee another franchise when one becomes available in the area. Even McDonald's competitors can see that this close scrutiny provides McDonald's with the industry's highest level of consistency."

The fact that organizational design can also pay dividends for governmental agencies was demonstrated in the medical aid program administered by Suffolk County, New York, on eastern Long Island. As was true for most federal, state, and local programs, Suffolk County had distributed responsibility for Medicaid assistance to a number of departments, chiefly those dealing with health and with social services.

Management recognized that the problems surfacing in Medicaid programs were chiefly of a financial control nature. The organizational solution to the problem was described by John V.N. Klein, County Executive:

"We put all Medicaid administration in a special medical assistance division of our Department of Social Services. . . . The responsibilities of our medical assistance division, which has a staff of over 160, include the screening of clients for eligibility and the constant examination of records to catch abuse and fraud, as well as overseeing the billing and payment of providers."

He went on to characterize the responsibility of this agency as doing:

". . . a positive job of making the system work for the needy. The poor and elderly are the least equipped to pick their way through the complex maze of regulations, forms, criteria, sections, and paperwork Medicaid imposes. Furthermore, the conscientious physician does not want to spend his or her time filling out forms and bills in quintuplicate."

Implementing this organizational design and associated management and operational controls reduced Medicaid expenditures by more than 20 percent from previously budgeted sums.

Clearly, then, management goals for quality of service are implemented through people relationships established by organizational design.

HOW DO YOU EXPLAIN SUCCESS?

When companies become highly successful, their achievements are frequently credited to marketing innovation, merchandising innovation, site selection, effective cost control, quality control, or other reasons. All of these attributes of success make real contributions.

K mart, for example, would not have been successful without an outstanding merchandising organization. Innovative marketing unquestionably contributed to success at McDonald's. Tight budgeting and operating controls undoubtedly contributed to improved earnings for Citibank.

However, all these strategies or programs depended upon and were achieved within effective organizational design. Results would not have been the same if these companies did not have effective organizational designs. In a retailing organization, for example, a marketing genius can only be effective in the long run if the organization is designed to implement and capitalize upon merchandising innovation. Without the presence of an effective organizational design, even the most creative and innovative merchandising programs will have a short-lived impact.

Examples abound where merchandising successes enjoyed only short durations because they were not supported organizationally. Consider, for example, the previously mentioned situation at E.J. Korvette. Other examples include Minnie Pearl's Chicken and W.T. Grant. In 1962, Grant and K mart were approximately the same size. One company concentrated on organization, the other on intensive sales programs of short duration.

WHAT IS THE ORGANIZATIONAL DESIGN PROCESS?

Effective organizational design for a service enterprise should face the potential for and eliminate some of the frustrations described in Chapter 2. This can be done in part through a design which concentrates upon:

1. Outcomes of customer satisfaction – as perceived from the customer's point of view
2. Imparting a sense of achievement and pride for employees rendering the service.

Let's recall some of the frustrations dealt with earlier:

- The hassle factor
- Inflation
- Defense of the status quo
- Devotion to process rather than results
- A propensity to allocate shortages rather than create new wealth
- A lack of commitment to customer satisfaction.

These, we feel, are the real issues with which organizational design must deal. It will not do to create organizational facades masking the same old bureaucracy. Many attempts by service entities to give consumers a personal sense of contact with the organization have been little more than facades. For example, consider a customer statement issued by a commercial bank which gives the name and phone number of a personal banker who can be called with problems. When this service is put to the test, it turns out that all the personal banker does is plug the customer into the same old bureaucracy. There is no organizational capability on the part of the personal banker to carry a transaction through from beginning to end or to satisfy a customer's inquiry.

We know of a credit card company which had a name and phone number printed on statements for customer reference. However, it developed that the name was fictitious. Customers who called the number were connected to the same operators sitting at the same computer terminals they had always used. It didn't take a complaining customer long to recognize the subterfuge.

By contrast, look at the growth which Allstate Insurance has realized by empowering salesmen in retail stores to handle complete service transactions with customers or prospective customers.

Organizational design should be a process for accomplishing customer satisfaction and for promoting motivation and pride among employees rather than being limited to acceptance and adoption of techniques currently in vogue. A process approach can be used without regard to management style. It doesn't matter whether the executive subscribes to Theory X, Theory Y, or a philosophy of participation or nonparticipation. Neither does the process approach subscribe to any particular technique or method for organization: functional, matrix, team, product management.

Rather, a process approach encompasses and leaves executives free to adopt or adapt any or all of these methods, as appropriate. The process approach, while based upon sound organizational development and behavioral theory, does not stress the theoretical basis but advocates a practical approach within each individual service enterprise.

The process approach to organizational design is applied at three levels within each organization:

1. The level at which the organization deals with its environment

2. The level at which the organizations within an enterprise deal with each other

3. The level at which individuals relate to the organizations of which they are a part.

WHERE DOES THE ORGANIZATIONAL DESIGN PROCESS COME FROM?

Most of the concepts which have been incorporated into the organizational design process described in this chapter have been adapted from concepts and writings put forward by the faculty of the Harvard Business School. In effect, the process described here represents a practical application of these concepts evolved through our experiences with operational companies.

In particular, we have used several of the organizational design concepts of Professors Paul R. Lawrence and Jay W. Lorsch of the Harvard Business School. Their work has been particularly innovative in its recognition of the need for companies to adapt the design of their plans of organization to the differences in their respective environments.

In their studies of successful organizations, Lawrence and Lorsch found that one of the major characteristics held in common was the manner in which the organizations related or were suited to their business environments. Lawrence and Lorsch call this type of environmental sensitivity the contingency theory of organization.

In looking at successful organizations in the service sector, we have, by inference, validated or substantiated this contingency theory. The successful organizations cited throughout this book have universally, through varying but effective means, adapted themselves to their environments. Conversely, the less successful organizations we have observed were not as sensitive to their environments.

We have also made heavy use of the work of Professor Anthony G. Athos of the Harvard Business School. He has had a strong impact on our thinking about how organizations compete through management policies covering the quality-productivity connection. Professor Athos has also been a strong influence in shaping our thinking about relationships between individuals and their organizations. His writings are reflected in a later section of this chapter, which deals with how organizations can cope with individuals.

HOW DOES AN ORGANIZATION
COPE WITH ITS ENVIRONMENTS?

This is the real question to be faced in dealing with the first identified level of organizational design – structuring the organization to do business with the outside world. This involves one of the basic, classic problems faced by managers – the division of labor. Once an organization becomes large enough so that the proprietor does not perform and deliver all services, management is faced with decisions on how to break down the total job so that it can be performed most effectively and efficiently.

In coping with the need for division of labor, many managers have focused on what we now believe to be the wrong problem. They have tended to view division of labor as a question of degree of centralization or decentralization. In our experience, this question is usually asked in the wrong context. Managers tend to think of the issue of centralization vs. decentralization in terms of their own relationships to the organizational unit being considered. Typically, if a manager feels the need to oversee a given unit personally, the tendency will be to centralize it. If the manager feels that personal supervision isn't necessary, the decision will usually be to decentralize. In either case, the reasons being considered are wrong, since they do not involve the results the organizational unit is expected to deliver or the environment within which it is operating.

Lawrence and Lorsch have developed what they call a differentiation-integration model for dealing with organizational design. These terms are highly abstract. However, the theories behind this model are proven and sound. We have found it useful to adapt them, practically if not precisely, for our work in organizational design of service enterprises.

The term *differentiation* as we interpret it, describes how an organization divides, or groups, its people to deal effectively with the outside world while meeting the objectives of the enterprise. Once the organization has divided itself into work groups to deal with the outside world, these organizational units need a way for dealing with each other. Lawrence and Lorsch call this *integration*. Integration is covered in later discussions on the level of organizational design dealing with relationships between internal groups.

HOW SHOULD MANAGEMENT THINK ABOUT DIVIDING THE ORGANIZATION TO DEAL WITH THE OUTSIDE WORLD?

Lawrence and Lorsch suggest, and we have found it useful, that managers look at the relative stability of the environment as a prime consideration in determining how an organization should differentiate itself – or set itself up to deal with its outside world. Stability, as we use the term, is a description of how fast the environment is moving or changing. Other factors include evaluations of how much is known about the environment, how predictable it is, how much managers can rely on feedback from sources within the environment, and the time span required for completing transactions. It may also be useful to think about markets, economic factors, the rate at which technology is developing, the degree of regulation, and the nature of competition. In addition, the nature of services demanded by the marketplace should also be considered.

Figure 6-3 illustrates differentiation of an organization. Individual segments of a business are assigned responsibility for interacting with specific elements of the marketplace. It becomes the responsibility of managers of these segments to identify and deal with their customers. Criteria for differentiation can vary with organizations. Market segments, for example, may be aligned according to industry, demographics, customer size, or geography.

In general, the greater the certainty and stability of an environment, the lower will be an organization's need to differentiate, or divide itself to cope with its environment. An organization serving a relatively homogeneous market with comparatively few, uncomplicated products will be able to organize itself simply, perhaps along functional lines, in dealing with its environment. On the other hand, an organization dealing with a rapidly changing, diverse, high-technology market would develop an organization with a high degree of division of labor, with numerous units set up to do business with the outside world.

The impact of environmental factors on service-industry organization structures can be seen with clarity in developments among commercial banks. Until comparatively recently, money-center commercial banks dealt chiefly with corporate

ORGANIZING ACCORDING TO
ENVIRONMENTAL DIFFERENCES

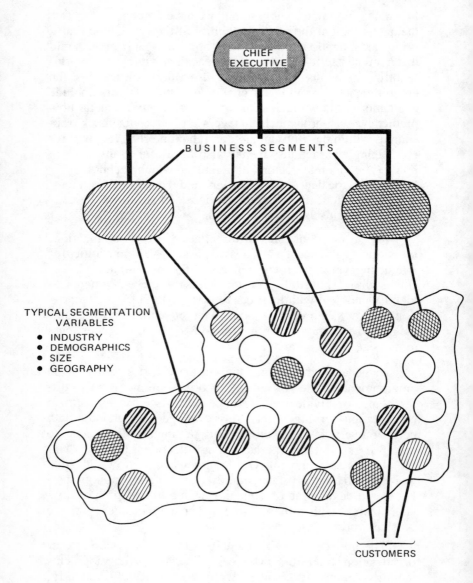

Figure 6-3

customers, principally large accounts. The credit environment in which they operated was relatively stable, uncomplicated, and not particularly fast moving.

Facing these conditions, virtually all commercial banks adopted a functional organization structure centered around their credit operations. In this environment, that approach represented a satisfactory division of labor. This was so because the nature of the environment was relatively stable, the products provided were generally low in complexity, and operating costs were comparatively fixed. In these circumstances, there was little demand for organizational changes aimed at optimizing quality of service and productivity. For many years in commercial banking, improvements in quality and productivity would not necessarily have represented competitive advantages.

In recent years, there have been marked changes in the environment within which commercial banks operate. Costs and availability of funds have changed rapidly. Operating costs have risen. There is competition from many new sources. Customer sophistication has grown. In other words, the once-stable market environment has become relatively unstable. In this changed environment, the quality of services rendered and the productivity realized in delivering them became major competitive factors. Accordingly, many large money-center banks reorganized themselves to conform to marketplace opportunities and corporate objectives.

In this period of accelerating change, Citibank and the Bank of America emerged as worldwide leaders as a result of innovative policies of organization for productive delivery of high-quality services. In California, the Bank of America enhanced its position as a retail-oriented bank specializing in consumer services through introduction of Bankamericard and other retail-type services. In New York City, Citibank improved service to its corporate clientele by organizing and delivering services according to the nature of large corporations or customer groups.

Both enterprises organized around their objectives, their basic beliefs about their roles – and around the emerging environments in which they found themselves. Both leapfrogged considerably ahead of their competitors. These successes, it is worth noting, did not stem from any significant differences in the services being offered, but from the way these two banks organized themselves to serve identified customers. Other banks in the same markets offered the same or similar products. These other banks, however, did not enjoy the same degree of success because they were organized differently. Citibank and Bank of America, in fact, competed through management policy.

WHAT CAN A SERVICE ENTERPRISE DO TO DIFFERENTIATE ITS ORGANIZATION?

The major thrust of organizational design for a service enterprise in a dynamic environment should be to link up its organization as tightly as possible with that environment. Citibank did this by organizing its corporate-service operations along geographic and industry lines. The concept was to have specialists capable of delivering quality services while realizing high levels of productivity.

This was accomplished by subdividing the organization, in effect, into a series of "minibanks" charged with serving targeted industries. Managers of these "minibanks" were encouraged to behave like entrepreneurs. They were free to decide what services would be rendered in their specialized markets. At the same time, however, they were responsible for realizing profits and for allocating the resources made available to them.

As an example, let's consider the relationship between Citibank and one of the major oil companies. This relationship falls within a World Corporation Group responsible for services to multinational companies. One of the "minibanks" set up within this group specializes in meeting the needs of energy industry companies. Within this "minibank," one of the subdivisions is a team specializing in services to this particular client. This organizational structure is diagrammed in Figure 6-4.

The relationship between Citibank and their client has been carried out to a level where bank people and equipment have been installed at client locations. Clearly, the objective is responsiveness. Citibank's client service team has been charged with developing the most effective and efficient ways for delivering the bank's total services to this major customer. The client service team, in turn, has responsibility and accountability for delivering these services productively and profitably.

ORGANIZING TO ACHIEVE INTEGRATION

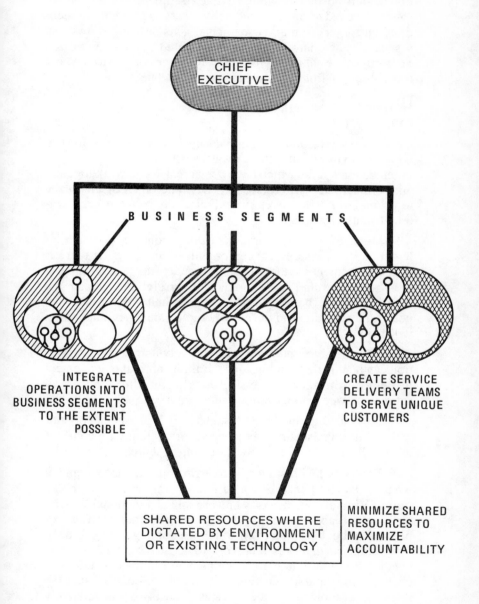

Figure 6-4

Figure 6-4 illustrates the concept of organizational integration within business segments. Each segment has all the resources needed to produce and deliver services directly to identified customers or market segments. This drawing shows that segments may share resources as required or that centralized pools may be established for major resources or services where technology or financial considerations dictate.

HOW DOES AN ORGANIZATION COPE WITH ITSELF?

Once an organization has adopted a division of labor to deal with its environments, there is a need to figure out how the organizational units which have been created can work together and communicate with each other. Lawrence and Lorsch use the term *integration* to cover the relationship between organizational units.

Management considerations center around how much integration is necessary between organizational units. If there is little requirement for these units to interact, the task of integration becomes relatively simple. Conversely, the greater the interdependence between organizational units, the greater the need for integration and the more complex the job of integration will be.

If the need for integration is relatively minor, an organization can handle the relationships within its normal management hierarchy. Managers make decisions about allocation of resources between organizational units as needs arise.

If the need for integration is relatively high, special organizational mechanisms may be needed for dealing with conflicts in establishing priorities and allocating resources.

This is easily illustrated by referring back to the example of what banks and banking looked like in simpler, less complex times. Virtually all banks were organized functionally, with divisions of labor covering credit, branch operations if appropriate, and bookkeeping or customer accounting. The degree of integration needed was relatively low. In most banks it was handled informally in conversations between the executives in charge of the separate functions. This could be done because the degree of complexity of the services themselves was relatively low. Customer requirements also tended to be on the simple, straightforward side. Thus, the need to tailor services to meet customer demands did not pose a major problem.

However, as the credit function of the bank is broken into multiple, market-oriented groups, the interdependencies between these units and the bookkeeping and customer accounting function become considerably more complex. The work of the customer accounting and bookkeeping function also becomes substantially more complex as it tries to keep up with the increasing numbers of divisions or groupings in its workload.

This increasing complexity within the bookkeeping function, in turn, presents a need for management with greater levels of sophistication. The customer accounting and bookkeeping support function can actually grow into a large, independent unit. Conflicts can emerge and multiply as this unit gains a life and identity of its own. This kind of situation abounded in banking during the sixties, when most commercial banks introduced large-scale computers for customer accounting.

Conflicts of organizational integration were minimized at Citibank by subdividing operational responsibilities to correspond with customer-service orientations. That is, the "minibanks" established to serve customers were set up as self-contained units with complete transaction processing capabilities. Each "minibank" could serve an individual customer or group of customers with almost complete independence, with little reliance on centralized facilities or services. This approach was facilitated by the minicomputer technology of the seventies, in contrast to the maxicomputer approaches of the sixties.

This degree of integration in organizational design yields both quality and productivity improvements because the same people responsible for services to the customer also gain the means for efficient and effective delivery of those services. The tests of the marketplace are, in effect, applied at the "minibank" level because the "minibanks" have to compete successfully if they are to survive.

HOW CAN AN ORGANIZATION COPE WITH INDIVIDUALS?

Management of an organization must recognize both its dependence upon the contributions of individuals and also the

needs of the individuals for motivators, which include opportunities for achievement, recognition, responsibility, advancement, growth, the need for affiliation, feedback, pride, and the
ability to make a contribution.

As indicated earlier, our thinking about the relationships
between individuals and their organization has been shaped by
the work of Professor Athos of the Harvard Business School.
Professor Athos has shared with us a model which represents a
framework for realizing outcomes of quality, productivity, and
profitability from individual contributions. A simplified version
of this model is presented in Figure 6-5.

MODEL OF SMALL, STABLE WORK GROUPS*

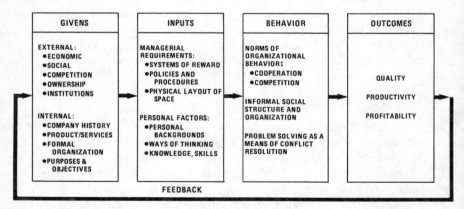

GIVENS	INPUTS	BEHAVIOR	OUTCOMES
EXTERNAL: ●ECONOMIC ●SOCIAL ●COMPETITION ●OWNERSHIP ●INSTITUTIONS INTERNAL: ●COMPANY HISTORY ●PRODUCT/SERVICES ●FORMAL ORGANIZATION ●PURPOSES & OBJECTIVES	MANAGERIAL REQUIREMENTS: ●SYSTEMS OF REWARD ●POLICIES AND PROCEDURES ●PHYSICAL LAYOUT OF SPACE PERSONAL FACTORS: ●PERSONAL BACKGROUNDS ●WAYS OF THINKING ●KNOWLEDGE, SKILLS	NORMS OF ORGANIZATIONAL BEHAVIOR: ●COOPERATION ●COMPETITION INFORMAL SOCIAL STRUCTURE AND ORGANIZATION PROBLEM SOLVING AS A MEANS OF CONFLICT RESOLUTION	QUALITY PRODUCTIVITY PROFITABILITY

FEEDBACK

*Source: "Note on stable work groups," a paper by Professor Anthony G. Athos, Harvard Business
School © 1974, President and Fellows, Harvard College.

Figure 6-5

We have found it particularly interesting to observe the representation by this model of the flow of actions required to achieve desired outcomes from contributions of individuals. For example, the issues of organizational structure discussed earlier in this chapter are found in the Athos model as "Givens." It is interesting also to observe that organizational designs have not really touched individual behavior and have not directly influenced desired outcomes for the organization. Professor Athos would suggest that management can deal with behavior only through the introduction and application of leadership skills.

The real challenge of leadership for service entities centers around the creation of an environment in which the factors of achievement, recognition, and the others mentioned above become the behavioral norms of the organization and all its individual contributors. The greater the success management enjoys in gaining acceptance for these factors, the greater the chance for achieving targeted outcomes of quality, productivity, and profitability. Conversely, as tasks are structured into highly functional, detailed, procedural sets of miniactivities, organizations generate assembly-line types of performance. These rarely fit into a service environment.

It is also true that motivation and quality of performance seem to increase as knowledge workers gain a role in the planning, as well as execution, of tasks assigned to them. Further, motivation increases with the scope of responsibilities. Performance improves where an individual is able to carry a task through from start to completion. Quality becomes even higher in situations where individuals or groups are encouraged by the nature of their work assignments to develop client relationships.

A way of working together for the delivery of services which we have read about frequently and have found effective in our own work is the so-called team approach. In this context, a team is a group of people working together to plan for and deliver services to a "client." The client could be an organization or individual within the same company or an outside customer of the enterprise.

The effectiveness of the team approach is well illustrated in the example of how Citibank serves the previously mentioned major oil company. The team was founded specifically to provide services right in the offices of the client. It is difficult to imagine a greater level of environmental sensitivity than an organizational design which calls for decentralizing right into the client organization.

The team approach achieves a number of important service-oriented advantages. Among these is the establishment of uniform goals and purposes for team members working together to serve the client. Feedback is immediate. Discrete, unique tailoring of certain services is virtually automatic. Quality of services, as perceived by client personnel working closely with team members, is invariably high. Productivity and efficiency are equally high because knowledge workers will find the best way to deliver the services needed without building in the hierarchy of inspection, control, and management functions needed to assure quality on assembly lines.

Our description of the elements of management policy as a means of competition for service organizations has thus been carried to the individual level. When individuals are made part of a team responsible for delivering quality services productively, each person becomes a competitor. Each individual assumes a role and responsibility as a member of a world-class team.

7
IMPLEMENTING THE ORGANIZATIONAL DESIGN

HOW DO YOU IMPLEMENT AN ORGANIZATIONAL DESIGN?

Any prospective change to an organization requires a program of implementation. This implementation program, in turn, requires specific, focused management attention. We have found it profitable to separate consideration of what is to be done from how it is to be accomplished.

Accordingly, this chapter is devoted to consideration of how to implement organizational design – as distinct from concerns for what an organization should look like, which was discussed in the last chapter. This content breakdown stresses that it can be profitable to put as much emphasis on how to accomplish a change as upon programs for deciding what is to be done.

Successful implementation of any management program or policy requires three basic elements:

1. Management commitment
2. Involvement or participation of those responsible for making the program work
3. Phasing – rate of absorption of change.

Management Commitment

The people involved in and responsible for the changes that will make an organization responsive to its environment and to management objectives have to be committed to the policy to be implemented. If managers have not thought through the concepts well enough to commit themselves without reservation, the organization is not ready to test or pilot the program on a limited basis. Test or pilot implementation of organizational plans is dangerous and generally unworkable if the concepts involved have not been considered thoroughly, and if potential problems and their solutions have not been anticipated. People are involved. People will be against any program which experiments with their lives and their futures. They want to feel that management knows what it's doing. They want to feel that there are good reasons for the changes they are being asked to take part in and that the new relationships established will be around for a while.

The commitment to change an organization has to come from the top downward. Organizational change cannot be a bottom-up process. Management at any level cannot expect organization elements below them to change without a prerequisite commitment that management itself will change. People have to be convinced that management has a good reason – that it is committed to meeting corporate objectives and/or to coping with the environment.

The apparent willingness and degree of commitment undertaken by top management is, in itself, a good measure of the prospective success of a program for organizational change. If the program cannot demonstrate a commitment at the top, and if it can't be defended at the top, the likelihood of overall success is low. Conversely, of course, an all-out, demonstrated management commitment enhances the likelihood of success.

A program for organizational change requires and consumes considerable energy. The necessary energy is released into the organization through demonstration of the need for change and of a commitment by management to support the change. This commitment has to be at a level and to an extent that will create a dissatisfaction with the status quo.

This dissatisfaction, in turn, helps to release the necessary energy and motivation to endure the pain and fear which are a part of any major program of change. Thus, without a convincing commitment, the probability of successful implementation of a program of change is reduced and the overall organization's ability to focus on management objectives is diminished.

Involvement

Change belongs to its achievers. People involved in bringing about the outcomes of a program of change acquire a proprietary attitude. They gain a feeling of accomplishment. When this feeling can be imparted to an organization, probabilities of success are greatly enhanced.

This is not to say that every individual within an organization being changed can be, or should be, consulted on the specifics of the program. However, enough people should be involved and should participate to be sure that the change can be made to work and that adequate organizational analysis has been performed. It never hurts to ask people: "What to you think?" Even if the answer is a surprise, something may be learned in the process. Similarly, it can be productive to ask: "How would you approach this problem or achieve this outcome?" Answers to such questions can lead to improvements over preconceived notions which precede them.

In our experience, a representative task force provides an excellent vehicle for implementing an organizational change. A task force, typically, involves people at all levels within the organization who are willing to commit the time and energy necessary to study issues constructively. Such a task force achieves a high degree of organizational involvement and acceptance. Its very existence and participation in a program serve to provide a high measure of support for the concepts to which management has been committed.

Several critical issues should be considered on formation of each task force. These include:

1. Objectives should be set for each task force formed. They should establish a mandate or charter within which the group operates.

2. The structure, membership, and leadership of the task force should be considered carefully to assure that all members realize a positive experience. Task forces should build people.

3. The end result or report to be completed by the task

force should be specified in advance. Planning should assure that the work of the task force will be closed out in an orderly way so as to avoid frustrations which come through lingering, low-productive duties after the main purpose has been concluded.

Support for the work of a task force is carried forward even after it has been disbanded and members returned to their regular organizational positions. Their presence within the organization provides a nucleus of people precommitted to the program of change. ·

Phasing – Rate of Absorption of Change

Changes involving people can proceed only so fast. There is a natural limitation upon the rate at which major organizational changes can be absorbed by the people responsible for implementing them. This is a human limitation.

The constraints or limits on how fast a new organizational design can be implemented will vary with the plan itself and with each individual group of people. The factors involved are behavioral. They must be estimated and monitored separately for the unique factors peculiar to each organization or major group.

Determining the rate of absorption is highly judgmental. Considerations are based on the complexity of the new responsibility being assumed and upon the relationships being established. Also bearing upon the rate of absorption is the degree to which the nature and culture of the organization are being altered. In estimating the rate of absorption, the higher the rate of involvement and participation achieved in the analysis and design of the new organization, the more rapid will be the rate at which change can be absorbed.

No matter how much involvement and participation there has been, however, there is still a limit to the speed with which organizations of people can be changed. There must be a specific sequence and timing worked out in advance. If the pacing of these events exceeds the ability of the organization to absorb the changes, the efforts involved will be wasted. If the pacing is too slow, the people will become impatient and the efforts may become counterproductive.

Above all, management impatience must be held in check. Many managers succumb to their impatience and try to implement major changes in one big swallow. This "big bath" approach to change doesn't alter the basic rate of absorption for any organization. If change is introduced faster than people can assimilate it, it doesn't happen. People gravitate to familiar patterns, doing what they know how to do rather than what somebody thinks they are supposed to do.

It is necessary to recognize that motivated, creative managers can always conceptualize organizational changes faster than people can implement them. One of the challenges of effective management lies in recognizing and projecting the necessary lead times, then living within them. Lasting organizational change takes years, not weeks or months. This can be a frightening prospect for a motivated, aggressive manager. But an insightful manager must recognize these conditions, use them to establish limitations on his or her own expectations, and adjust accordingly.

We have often heard it said that: "If we can put a man on the moon, why can't we improve the way we do things around here?" The reasoning behind such a question is fallacious. The question itself is irrelevant. Putting a man on the moon was a project effort. There was no existing organization to change. Human behavior did not have to be altered. Further, the commitment behind this specific project was unique – certainly nothing which could be reproduced in the average business environment.

A change involving the objectives and behavior of a service organization is far more extensive in terms of organizational impact than putting a man on the moon. Although it is certainly far less technical in terms of behavioral objectives, it is actually more complex. If this were not the case, the war on poverty could have been won years ago simply by assembling a team of dedicated experts.

Phasing breaks down the tasks that have to be completed in organizational change into "chewable bites." That is, phasing creates a series of steps which are understandable and manageable for implementation by the organization's people.

Let's illustrate this with a situation where an organization wishes to establish client-service teams. The creation and initiation of operations for a single team would represent a phase in the implementation of a new organizational design. In the course of completing this initial phase, management will identify and develop an understanding of the implementation problems which lie ahead with other team units.

In effect, this type of phasing presents an opportunity to try out the whole concept of the team approach before involving large numbers of people. This gives the organization all the potential benefits of testing or piloting without exposure to the disadvantages or uncertainties of these techniques. Problems are identified and bugs are worked out as the program of change is implemented.

Such phasing also creates the obvious benefit of positive feedback. Once the first team phase is successful, word gets around. Confidence builds. Success becomes contagious. The program for change is presold throughout the rest of the organization, which becomes energized to make the new organizational design work.

WHERE DOES THIS LEAD US NOW?

No matter how effective, efficient, or responsive an organizational design may be, it can still fall short of meeting its projected outcomes if provision has not been made for ongoing monitoring and management. Without advance planning for ongoing management, it is possible to have an organization which, literally, is running out of control.

As a general rule, the greater the division of labor to be built into an organization (differentiation), and the lower the rate of integration required, the more essential it becomes to overlay the organizational structure with management controls. Thus, once it has been decided how an organization is to be structured, it becomes essential, before any implementation takes place, to plan for the controls which will monitor the altered organization. The concepts and techniques for establishing these management controls are introduced in the next chapter.

8
MANAGEMENT CONTROL

WHAT IS MANAGEMENT CONTROL?

Even in the best run organizations, management control is the most often overlooked necessity of effective management. Most frequently, it is a missing link between organizational design and operational control. This is why we have presented the three elements of management policy as a set, rather than as a series of pieces.

Within this context, management control forms the link between plans, including organizational design, and the operational (or productive) means for achieving such plans, operational controls. The most meaningful definition we have found for management control has been framed by Professor Robert N. Anthony of the Harvard Business School, whose writings are preeminent in this area. This definition was paraphrased in Chapter 5. As a basis for this discussion, it is worth quoting in full:

> "*Management control* is the process by which managers assure that resources are obtained and used effectively and efficiently in the accomplishment of the organization's objectives."

It is also worth repeating within the context of this definition that the term *effectively* means that resources are applied in the right places. The term *efficiently* means that they are secured at the lowest feasible cost. Professor Anthony stipulates further that this definition implies that the process involves managers – "people who get things done by working with other people" – and that "the process takes place within a context of objectives and policies that have been arrived at in the strategic planning process."

In calling management control a process, we identify it as a series of actions which, when completed, leads to a specified result. For management control, that specified end result is the achievement of the objectives of the organization. Management control should form a dynamic, living element of management policies and programs. Management control is something greater than and different from a management information system. It must involve more than the presentation of information.

Experienced managers find it easy to identify with the need for designing an organization to meet objectives, to serve its environment, and to produce given outcomes. It is also easy to identify with the need for tight operational controls over business transactions. There is a tendency to think that if you have a soundly designed organization and controls over your business transactions, you have all the management tools you need. This isn't the case. A system of management control is necessary. All too often, this is missing.

Without management controls to fill this potential void, an organization could conceivably have what it perceives to be an excellent service effectively delivered while, in reality, a base of dissatisfied customers is being built. Admittedly, this type of phenomenon could not last long. But, depending on the state of the economy at any given moment, it could last long enough to kill an organization.

HOW MUCH MANAGEMENT CONTROL DOES A SERVICE ENTERPRISE NEED?

Even though it is a necessary link between strategic and organizational plans on one side and operational controls on the other, management controls need not be highly formalized, documented, or rigidly structured. Rather, management controls should be just formal and structured enough so that responsible management is comfortable with them. The degree of formality of any system of management control will vary with the complexity of both the organization structure and the operational control system. Management controls should establish a level of detail with which responsible managers are comfortable.

To illustrate, a manager who has grown up through an operational control system to a position of responsibility may very well feel that a relatively informal, unstructured system of reporting is sufficient. Specific needs for such a person would depend on the extent of change which had taken place since the individual left the operational environment.

For example, a merchandising executive who has been a salesperson, a buyer, and has grown into a position as vice president or general merchandising manager may have acquired an intuitive "feel" for management control. Such a person might think that a formalized system was unnecessary.

Possibly, however, this person's intuition may have become obsolete. Also, the individual's experience base may not have the span necessary to encompass all of the elements of planning, feedback, and control necessary to assure that resources are being allocated effectively to meet the objectives of the· organization.

In fact, such instincts may be more of a liability than an asset. Intuition has locked many managers into a downward-looking posture where they remain preoccupied with operational details rather than looking upward toward the strategic aspects of their jobs. The literature of business management is full of examples of executives who could not make the transition from tactical to strategic thinking and decision making.

HOW DO COMPANIES COMPETE THROUGH MANAGEMENT CONTROL?

To answer this question, we return to our basic premise: service organizations compete primarily through management policy dealing with the quality-productivity connection. Management control is an element of management policy. Therefore, management control is an element of the competitive stance taken by an enterprise.

The state of the art in the development of management controls for service entities is much the same as that discussed in the previous chapter on organizational design. That is, a lot is known, and a lot has been done, in the manufacturing area. Comparatively little management expertise has been developed or applied specifically for service enterprises.

As is the case for organizational design, it is necessary for a service entity to develop management controls which meet the requirements of its particular customers. Management controls must conform to the unique demands associated with the delivery of services, as distinct from the production of products. Ultimately, a management control system should be designed to assure that the organization's profitability is achieved through the rendering of quality services productively.

Given the elements of competition, quality of service, and productivity which govern success for a service enterprise, a key characteristic of management controls in this environment should be that they anticipate the market conditions. The management controls should look forward, not backward. To contribute to the competitive success of the organization, management controls should measure quality as perceived by customers and should monitor productivity in comparison with objectives and past performance. The same management controls should also focus on the dollar profitability of the enterprise.

These, of course, are not the only requirements for management controls; they are just the elements which bear upon capabilities to compete. Within this concern for competitive success, management controls should constitute an early warning system which sets off alarms any time standards for quality or productivity are not being met. Declines in quality and productivity, after all, precede and signal changes in market share and/or profitability.

In addition, since people constitute the most critical resource and the actual delivery system for a service enterprise, management controls should measure how well this resource is being employed. Criteria to be monitored in the personnel area should include turnover, productivity, growth, and job satisfaction.

We have not seen a successful service enterprise which lacked a management control system, either formal or informal.

HOW ABOUT SOME EXAMPLES OF MANAGEMENT CONTROL FAILURE?

An excellent illustration of a management control failure can be seen in a further look at the example in Chapter 3, describing the retail department store organization which experienced a decline following reorganization.

This company had advanced strategic thinkers at the top level and sound, practical operational thinkers involved in its operational controls. In between, there was a void. As a result, the strategies and organization of the enterprise went one way, operations another. The management control which would have formed a link was missing.

To illustrate, departmental organization is a basic focal point for retailing management. At the operational level, merchandising takes place at the classification, item, or stockkeeping unit (SKU) level. In between, merchandising conceptualization – a determination of what products, sizes, colors, etc., a market will buy – takes place at the departmental management level. It requires a management control process to provide a tool for measuring the effectiveness and the efficiency of the department, particularly in terms of that unit's profit contribution to the organization. In the case cited, this was a sorely missed link.

Other missing links in the management control process included the collection and reporting of information on the market share enjoyed by each department. Further, the void between strategy and operations produced a break, or obstacle, to the professional growth of employees. People are critical resources in any service enterprise. Planning for and monitoring of the development of people is a vital element of management control. This element was missing.

An example of a management control for measuring quality of service as perceived by customers can be seen in methods used by a major financial services institution to test new products and the effectiveness of advertising. This organization routinely samples a population of 2,000 established customers and 2,000 non-customers to evaluate reactions to new products or advertising programs.

A standing management group, the investor committee, has been given continuing responsibility for applying this management control. Through these efforts, the company's marketing programs – and customer satisfaction – are tested continuously.

The same kind of feedback is invited by a number of quality hotel chains, which leave questionnaires in guest rooms and conduct separate surveys to measure customer satisfaction continuously. The program of Western International Hotels for continuing inspection of company properties is a good example of quality consciousness in the hotel industry.

Although individual facilities are managed with a high degree of autonomy, a centralized quality-control function has been set up to monitor customer satisfaction and standards of operating quality. Teams of experienced managers monitor everything from waiting lines in the lobbies to the servicing of rooms with towels, soap, linens, and amenities. This is done continuously, with measurement reported against established standards. Any deterioration in performance is used as a signal to indicate required management action.

Opportunities to monitor and improve quality of service are not confined to private, profit-motive entities. Governmental organizations, particularly at the local or regional level, have also been able to improve productivity and reduce costs to taxpayers through programs aimed primarily at the upgrading of quality of services. For example, the Suffolk County program cited in Chapter 6 included management controls for screening clients for eligibility and examining records to identify cases of abuse and fraud. These management controls were given primary credit for a turnaround in Medicaid costs. In 1977, the Medicaid budget established for Suffolk County was $100.7 million, up substantially from $48.2 million in 1973, $57 million in 1974, and $86.3 million in 1976 despite the fact that the eligible population remained about the same. Actual expenditures for 1977 came to approximately $77.6 million.

Just as effective management control can have positive effects, a lack of management controls, or inappropriate controls, can have negative effects. To illustrate, we can cite the case of a major bank which measures quality of transaction processing in terms of errors per thousand items. This is an internal, operational type of measurement. It does not look at services from a customer's standpoint. An organization which relies on this type of measurement to insure quality might well be rendering deteriorating services without the awareness of its management. This is because it is measuring the wrong things. For instance, a multimillion dollar transfer of funds would be measured under the same criteria, according to this sytem, as the processing of personal checks. Clearly, customers do not regard the transactions in the same way.

WHAT IS THE MANAGEMENT CONTROL PROCESS?

Professor Anthony, who has developed the most workable definition for management control we have encountered, has also, in our belief, done the best job of describing what the process of management control should include. As seen by Professor Anthony, a management control process is a framework for thinking about ways to assure that "resources are obtained and used effectively and efficiently in the accomplishment of the organization's objectives."

A graphic representation of Professor Anthony's framework is shown in Figure 8-1. A key conceptual point to note in this diagram is the realistic positioning of management control in its relationship to strategic planning and operational control. Further, information handling and financial accounting systems are shown as loosely related processes which are external to management control considerations.

It is important to recognize, as Professor Anthony does, the differences between the processes represented in the framework. It would be impossible, in our opinion, to design a single system to integrate all of the elements represented in this framework.

In using the illustration in Figure 8-1, and in citing Professor Anthony's book, we hope to highlight the fact that this discussion is not intended as a set of directions on how to design and implement management controls. Rather, our interest lies in how management control techniques, implemented with readily available knowledge, can be applied to help create a system of management which assures quality and productivity for service enterprises.

WHAT RESOURCES ARE CONTROLLED?

The definition of management control which we are supporting stresses that this is a system for obtaining and using resources.

PLANNING AND CONTROL PROCESSES IN ORGANIZATIONS

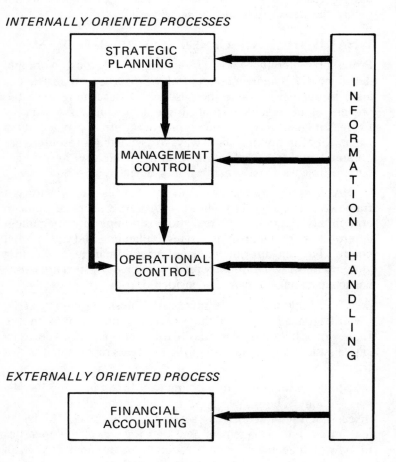

Source Robert N. Anthony, *Planning and Control Systems:*
A Framework for Analysis, Harvard School of Business
Administration, Harvard University, p. 22.

Figure 8-1

In defining what a management control system is, it is desirable to identify the resources commonly employed in service entities to achieve management objectives. These include:

- People
- Capital
- Customers and markets
- Current assets (including accounts receivable, cash, and inventories).

People, as a resource, establish the competitive differences between organizations. People also represent the resource through which services are actually delivered. Management controls should anticipate the extent of people resources required and monitor the performance of the organization in employing these resources.

The need for and function of *capital* as a resource for service enterprises is demonstrated easily by the current "urge to merge" among investment bankers. In this industry, Merrill Lynch has by far the strongest capital position. Capital resources have unquestionably been used effectively by Merrill Lynch to enhance its competitive position. By comparison, other investment banking firms are having to merge to aggregate enough capital to compete.

Capital formation is possibly the most critical requirement faced by investment bankers. Capital is needed to finance investments in inventories of securities, to finance new products or services, and to expand distribution networks.

Similarly, health care has also become a capital-intensive industry. Tremendous investments are currently being made in new facilities and equipment. Efficient utilization of capital resources among health care organizations has become a critical management control issue within this industry.

Classifying capital as a key resource for a service organization may fly in the face of conventional wisdom which holds that service firms are not capital intensive. Today, we feel it is more accurate to say that service enterprises are only now beginning to recognize the need to improve their return on capital.

Customers and markets are not conventionally considered as resources to be employed in management of an enterprise. However, in dealing with a service environment, we have found it helpful to think of customers and markets as resources to be served. More specifically, customers and markets provide key criteria upon which management controls are based. Customer service standards, market share, and productivity should, we feel, be regarded as elements within the framework of this "resource."

A real management control challenge lies in the velocity with which *current assets* such as inventories and accounts receivable can be converted to cash, and the rate at which cash can be put to work profitably. These management control criteria result partly from today's costs of money. Also important, however, are the relatively short-lived and perishable natures of service industry assets in inventories and accounts receivable. There are few things more perishable than an unused service or an unpurchased item of fashion inventory. Similarly, accounts receivable for services cannot be repossessed in the same way as a fungible manufactured item. Thus, uncollected receivables deteriorate faster for service enterprises than they do in other sectors.

WHAT ARE THE ELEMENTS OF MANAGEMENT CONTROL?

Management control has four elements, all of which are applied within a context which includes the structures and objectives of an organization:

1. Establishment of plans
2. Feedback on performance in comparison with plans
3. Control mechanisms for corrective action on the basis of feedback
4. A system of rewards.

Figure 8-2 illustrates the continuity of relationship between these four elements of management control.

An excellent discussion of the various elements of management control is found in the book, *Profitability Accounting* (Ronald Press, 1972), written by two Touche Ross partners,

THE ELEMENTS OF MANAGEMENT CONTROL

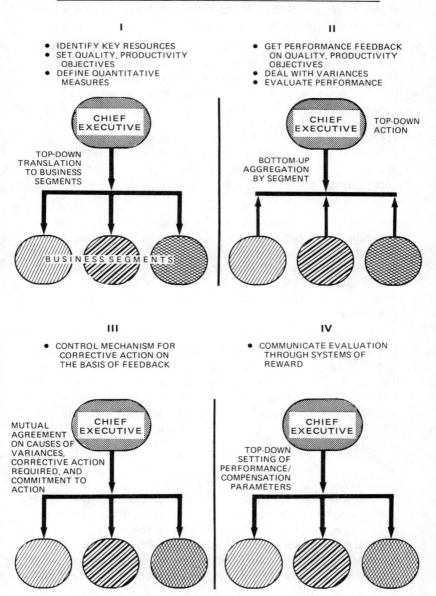

Figure 8-2

Robert Beyer and Donald J. Trawicki. This work is particularly strong in its treatment of the need to establish corrective actions to overcome unfavorable variances.

Management plans for a service entity must reflect and be built around the enterprise's objectives, the organizational structure adopted to meet them, and the resources allocated for this purpose. Plans must be established at an organizational, or responsibility, level by managers who will be accountable for realizing projected outcomes. To the extent possible, all plans should be quantified on the basis of a common denominator – dollars. Dollar outcomes should be specified wherever this is at all possible, including in budgets, plans for productivity gains, market share, return on investment, and profits.

Any effective management control system must report on results realized in comparison to plan. Variances between actual and planned results must be stated in terms that can be explained and acted upon readily. This feedback need not necessarily be immediate or in "real time." But results should be known quickly enough so that corrective action can be taken where appropriate.

There must be some vehicle within a management control system to trigger action on expectations and variances. Corrective mechanisms may be as simple as direct meetings between managers and subordinates. Or they may be as complex as extensive sets of written instructions for dealing with variances. This doesn't matter. The real point is that variances don't take care of themselves. They don't go away without corrective action.

One effective management control technique for assuring effective and efficient use of resources is to incorporate a system of monetary rewards. We believe a system of rewards should be an integral part of each enterprise's management controls. Further, the size of rewards should be based on the success of each responsible manager in attaining his or her performance objectives. This applies whether a system of rewards involves deferred compensation, some form of current income, or other incentives.

Rewards should be individualized and incremental on the basis of the contribution of people toward the meeting of the organization's objectives. To the extent possible, a system of rewards should recognize that each individual is paid to do a basic job. Incentives should reflect performance over and above this basic responsibility. They should be incremental, reflecting the degree to which actual performance exceeds the requirements of basic responsibilities.

It is also important to identify and separate the rewards realized by performers and non-performers in an organization. There is nothing more demoralizing to high achievers than an egalitarian pay system. This has been a key problem in motivating employees in the public sector. But it is not limited to public-sector entities. Many service companies, including insurance firms, banks, and retailers, have not provided sufficient incentive to stimulate champion-caliber performances.

Performance incentives should apply at all levels – not exclusively to management. A service organization tends to be structured horizontally for delivery of services to identified markets. This means that hierarchical controls common in organizations structured for product delivery are frequently not present in a service entity.

Since a service organization depends upon non-managerial people to play key roles in its delivery system, personnel other than managers should be qualified for incentive payment. This is basic to the nature of service jobs. The best manager may also be the best performer. But this is not always true; the best performer may not be the best manager. Therefore, the system of rewards should not require a nonproductive "promotion" to qualify people for attractive levels of compensation.

Incentives for line-type performance are frequently associated with commissioned positions. However, compensation programs should not be limited to such jobs. For example, a bank loan officer or account executive may properly not be in a position to receive commissions. But each individual should be paid for contributions made to achievement of the objectives of the enterprise and of the individual position. Both the service organization and its effective management controls must recognize and reward the contributions of nonmanagers who render services which are the end products of the organization.

HOW DO YOU IMPLEMENT
MANAGEMENT CONTROLS?

The same elements cited in the last chapter as requirements for any management program or policy apply to management control just as they do to organizational design:

1. Management commitment
2. Involvement or participation of those responsible for making the program work
3. Phasing – rate of absorption of change.

Management Commitment

Management control is a top-down process, one which derives its impetus from organizational design and strategic plans. To implement a top-down process, it is necessary that the organization's highest-level executives commit themselves to and support the philosophy under which they manage – as distinct from becoming involved in day-to-day transactions.

Effective management controls should give a top manager confidence that subordinates are on top of those aspects of the operation considered to be important. Managers should watch feedback on results, rather than concentrating on specific actions of subordinates. Management is implemented through reliance on information feedback. Management confidence comes from knowing what is happening, rather than supervising specific actions or operations.

The commitment to management control must be felt by all persons with responsibilities for realizing the organization's objectives and outcomes. Each responsible manager must be able to internalize and identify with the plans, feedback criteria, control mechanisms, and system of rewards associated with the management controls.

Putting it another way, management control is not – and should not be permitted to become – a system designer's dream-come-true. It should be a tool with which responsible managers can feel involved and comfortable. Design and implementation of management controls, therefore, cannot be delegated to established technical processes. Every involved manager must feel that he or she is part of the management control processes.

Involvement

Since people are critical to management controls, it follows that the people who will use them should be heavily involved in their development. This is not to say that managers must be the actual developers of controls. But we do intend to stress that users of controls must interact closely with the developers to assure that their needs are met – that their requirements are not subordinated to demands of equipment or preconceived notions of technicians.

It is unlikely, at least in the short run, that the very presence of management controls will change the management styles of the people using them. However, it is likely that the controls will become learning devices that promote professional growth in affected managers. This is true as long as the controls are flexible and responsive. This will not happen if a set of controls, once implemented, is regarded as "sunk in concrete" and unchangeable. Control elements must be changeable and adaptable as management's ability and willingness to use them increases.

Phasing – Rate of Absorption of Change

Given the top-down nature of management controls, it follows that they should be implemented in stages from the top down. Implementation takes place in varying degrees of detail, depending upon needs of managers at the various levels and in the various phases of implementation.

To illustrate, reporting on an organization's performance at the board-of-directors level may be implemented quickly and simply because of the relatively minor amount of detailing involved. This level may represent one phase of implementation. This initial phase could, in turn, be followed by phases structured according to segments of a business or divisions, as well as levels of the organization. Each downward cut at performance reporting may represent a separate implementation phase – and a pause in implementation to give managers a chance to become accustomed to the use of their new tool.

As acceptance of management controls takes place, user confidence builds – as long as the information provided is accurate, consistent, and reliably reported.

It is extremely important to recognize that a phase in the implementation of a set of management controls is entirely different from a hierarchical pyramid of data distilled from bottom-up summaries of business transactions. A transaction processing system, as will be demonstrated in the next chapter, is a different entity altogether. Links between transaction processing and management control reporting should, at most, be informal. There are more differences than similarities between management control and transaction processing.

WHERE DOES THIS LEAD US NOW?

Management control sets the stage for operational control. Management plans, programs, objectives, performance measures, decision rules, and operational parameters are carried out by transaction processing systems. Within our management system, we identify these transaction processing methods as part of an operational control system. Decision rules and other controls over transaction processing are built into operational control systems as repeatable functions. Therefore, operational control systems are highly programmatic in nature. The concepts and techniques for these operational controls form the subject matter for the next chapter.

9
OPERATIONAL CONTROL

WHAT IS OPERATIONAL CONTROL?

"Operational control is the process of assuring that specific tasks are carried out effectively and efficiently."

This definition is offered by Professor Anthony in the same book on planning and control systems cited previously. With this definition, Professor Anthony distinguishes between the performance of tasks under operational control and the utilization of resources under management control.

Within our context, operational control is the third of the three elements of the management system we feel essential for realizing both quality and productivity within a service entity.

As another characteristic, we mentioned earlier that operational control is both a process and a product. It is a process because of the continuity of tasks involved. It is a product because the operational control tasks frequently constitute the actual service delivered to customers. In other words, operational control encompasses the actual, day-to-day running of the business. Operational controls are essential to the successful conduct of any business.

HOW DO COMPANIES COMPETE
THROUGH OPERATIONAL CONTROL?

Companies compete through operational control because this area provides the first line of manageability for both quality and cost. Operational controls are where quality is built into the service rendered. Operational controls are also the points where costs can be taken out of the performance of a service.

Both quality and productivity are achieved because operational control actually becomes the working environment for the people rendering services. That is, operational controls determine the degree of repetitiveness, tedium, and boredom built into service industry jobs. To the extent that these jobs can be mechanized or computer controlled, there are frequently opportunities to enhance reliability of performance while reducing costs – as well as the likelihood of human error and the need for inspection or supervision.

Companies also compete in this management area because operational controls are a point of impact where problems become apparent. By the same token, if an organization is to deliver services responsibly, this is where management must be applied.

To avoid giving the impression that operational controls are some kind of panacea, let's establish a perspective. This point has not been introduced before. But, within this context, it is worth noting that service enterprises deliver two distinct types of end products. First, there is the transaction-based service – the kind rendered by banks, insurance companies, restaurants, hotels, and so on. Next there is the time-based service – in which providers sell increments of time rather than specific performances or units of product. To illustrate, time-based services can include medical services or professional services of attorneys and accountants.

The management system proposed in this book deals only with transaction-based services. Frankly, we do not know – and have not seen any evidence that management sciences in general know – how to devise a system for management and control of time-based services. In fact, it was just recently that we came across a document calling attention to this distinction between types of services. We encountered this conceptual insight in the text of a speech presented by Paul G. Hines, a Vice President of E.F. Hutton.

The competitive impact and value of operational controls over transaction-oriented services is easily illustrated. Consider, for example, the Cash Management Account (CMA) currently being promoted by Merrill Lynch. This is an operational control system which has had the effect of packaging a series of consumer finance-type services for extension of customer margin accounts. This expanded service makes it possible for Merrill Lynch to compete much more effectively with other investment bankers all over the country.

In another financial example, a number of commercial money-market banks are using operational controls competitively through the introduction of corporate cash management systems. Under these plans, terminals linked directly into bank computers are being installed in the offices of corporate clients. Financial officers of customer companies are acquiring direct control over their money-management transactions.

Also in the financial area, an operational control system has made it possible for American Express to combine and expand potential for two separate, longstanding services. This has been done by widespread installation of vending machines for traveler's checks. As a result, traveler's check business is expanded while an additional, valuable use has been established for the credit card.

The same rationale has been applied in retail banking through introduction of the Citicard. This is an embossed plastic card which can be used with conventional imprinters or can be read on special laser terminals. When the card was initially distributed, Citibank offered a single, introductory application – account balance reference. Since then, use of the card has been extended for check guarantees in thousands of retail establishments, for credit use, for debit use, and for operation of an expanding population of automatic teller machines. Ultimately, as the market develops, Citibank will have the technology in place to implement electronic funds transfer systems.

Competition through operational controls seems to us to represent a major area of opportunity for managers of service enterprises. In reviewing the full spectrum of transaction-based services, it becomes apparent that some industries, and some institutions, have been more successful than others in applying modern technology and operational control methods.

Among the success stories, we would include most commercial banks, personal loan companies, computer service companies, utilities generally, and some retailers. The common denominators in these industries have been the emergence of transaction systems in which the experiences of customers, employees, the service organizations, and associated management supervision are all integrated closely – on a timely basis. Characteristics of customer satisfaction tend to center around promptness, uniformity, and reliability of services rendered.

By contrast, the greater the variables in customer services, and the more people-dependent and labor intensive a service becomes, the less use companies seem to have made of advanced technology in their operational control systems. This is illustrated by comparatively low levels of sophistication and effectiveness of operational control systems we have observed in such industries as hotels, restaurants, auto rentals, securities brokers, and some retailers.

We perceive the lesser degree of sophistication in these areas as representing an opportunity for improvement rather than an inherent problem. This is illustrated by the transitions to improved operational control systems taking place in some industries, such as retailing, restaurants, and hotels. Consider the advanced state of operational systems in the fast food segment of the restaurant industry. In many McDonald's outlets, counter personnel use sales registers in which they simply touch points on a matrix keyboard to order menu items. The machines automatically display customer orders and total the purchase. Accuracy and speed have been improved. Pencil-and-paper entries have been eliminated. The introduction of such systems underscores opportunities to compete effectively through upgrading of operational control systems.

WHAT IS THE OPERATIONAL CONTROL PROCESS?

The operational control process is really a system for task processing. Its end result should be satisfactorily processed, individual transactions performed in a timely, reliable, and predictable way.

WHAT IS THE MANAGEMENT SIGNIFICANCE OF OPERATIONAL CONTROL?

If we say that operational control is a process involving a series of activities which lead to a specified result, it follows that the management challenge in this area lies primarily in planning, developing, and implementing the process, rather than detailed concern with day-to-day operations. If planning, development, and implementation steps are effectively managed, the ongoing operation of a system will become natural and routine to the organization. Thus, it seems appropriate to review briefly the areas of planning, development, implementation and operation.

Planning

Operational control was described earlier as a bottom-up process which takes its direction from a system of management control. Therefore, it is difficult, if not impossible, to develop an operational control system without having a fairly precise definition of the management controls within which it will function.

Consequences from lack of management definition have plagued the development of computerized systems in many companies and industries. A classic complaint from computer technicians or system designers has been that management really doesn't know what it wants from the system. To illustrate, it would be extremely difficult to design an operational control system for retail inventory management if inventory policies and decision criteria have not been defined in advance.

Yet, in our observation, many systems have been, and continue to be, designed in just this way. Organizations can get away with this type of practice in the operational control area primarily because most new operational control systems are simply automating tasks already being performed by other means.

We believe the key issue in operational control planning is the need for a link between an organization's management control and operational control processes. This link helps assure integrated management. As discussed previously, this is because effective management control should be closely aligned with the overall design of the organization. Therefore, an operational control system compatible with management controls will also be compatible with the structure of its organization.

The value of this integration between operational controls and the processes of management control and organizational design are easily illustrated: picture an organization which has been decentralized to conform to its markets or other external factors. Assume also that the organization has aligned its support functions to conform to this organizational structure. If this enterprise maintained or installed a large, monolithic transaction processing system, the complexities of integrating it into the organization would be immense because operational controls would be in conflict with organizational design. It would be extremely difficult to impose centralized processing on an organization decentralized to conform to its markets.

This is not intended to advocate decentralization of operational controls as the only approach to follow. Rather, the point to be stressed is that operational controls must be planned and implemented to conform to the design of the organization. The organization should not be expected to adjust itself to demands of operational controls. Failure to recognize this requirement is, we have noticed, a prevalent pitfall in the design of operational control systems.

The economics of computer processing today increasingly favor the use of mini or microcomputers which integrate transaction processing right into the user organization. Therefore, the alignment of operational controls to conform to the design of the organization is considerably simpler than it was a decade or so ago. This trend will continue.

In planning for operational control systems, however, it must also be recognized that offsetting problems have resulted. Specifically, in solving the technical problems of integration of computer processing into user organizations, entirely new sets of difficulties are introduced. For example, an organization is faced with the operation of multiple computer locations, multiple access points to the information assembled by computer systems, and a need for a greater number of more highly trained people. Planning for operational control systems, therefore, must recognize and deal with these new requirements.

Development and Implementation

Management concerns in the development of an operational control system should center around the need for defining the quality of outputs to be realized so as to demand quality in system design and end-result outputs. This applies even to development of a so-called "simple" minicomputer-based operational control system. Every transaction, in each system, has to be processed properly every time – from the customer's point of view. The developmental process, therefore, should reflect and provide for the needs of the customer, as well as for those of the internal user of a system.

This developmental requirement is unique to the service sector. In manufacturing and other industries, for example, the operational control system seldom affects or concerns customers directly. To illustrate, the buyer of an automobile has no impact upon or knowledge of the quality of the manufacturer's inventory management system. By contrast, a service customer is part of the operational control system. The customer writes the check, stands at the cash register, or interacts with an automated teller machine. The customer is right there, involved in and acutely aware of any problems. Therefore, techniques which served well to develop transaction processing systems in product-oriented industries are not transferable to service entities. A service organization must develop its operational control systems to conform to customer requirements.

Success in adapting operational control systems to customer needs requires carefully thought out developmental procedures and methods. Each system need not be an individual work of art. Rather, there should be consistency between systems. Development should be under controlled circumstances. While it may be a good idea organizationally to permit a user group to design its own minicomputer system, such practices should be carried out under established controls and standards.

Failure to direct system development to assure consistency and compatibility presents many problems, including the inability to transfer information from one system to another, the lack of ability to apply operational systems to multiple groups or organizational units, and the obvious problems of difficulties in maintenance and reliability which are inherent in non-standard designs. Frequently, we have observed, decentralized design leads to decentralized chaos. This is often one of the arguments put forward for centralized control over design and development. The argument can be overcome if decentralized development is carried out under a management system which assures standardization of design.

Operation

In operating a system to deliver services, it is critically important to remember that people are the key resource. The needs and requirements of operating employees – as well as those of customers – should be reflected in the design of an operating control system. The management requirements in integrating knowledge workers into an organization were discussed earlier, in the chapter on organizational design. There, it was recognized that it is necessary to design an organization to accommodate the needs of individual employees.

These approaches are worth re-emphasis in considering the operational requirements of service delivery systems. Such concepts as team building, multiple-task job assignments, and recognition for quality and productivity of performance must all be incorporated into the operational aspects of a system. People should drive the system; the system should not drive the people. With knowledge workers, the operational control system should encourage and permit each individual to find his or her own best way to deliver services.

HOW DO YOU IMPLEMENT AN OPERATIONAL CONTROL SYSTEM?

As with organizational design and management control, successful implementation of an operational control system requires three basic elements:

1.   Management commitment
2.   Involvement or participation of those responsible for making the program work
3.   Phasing – rate of absorption of change.

The management benefits which can result from integration of these three elements in the implementation of an operational control system, are well illustrated with the Cash Management Account (CMA) service of Merrill Lynch, described earlier. A program for the design, development, and introduction of this new product was the responsibility of Dennis Hess, Vice President for Product Development at Merrill Lynch. Mr. Hess told us recently that the planning, development, and implementation of CMA was entirely a "line activity." This is true even though he himself has what could be considered a staff position. Within the project for CMA development, he took on a line role, working closely and directly with system users. This made possible the management commitment and organizational involvement necessary for successful implementation. Contributing to this successful implementation was a phased program which permitted orderly introduction of the new product.

Management Commitment

The need for and nature of management commitment for the implementation of programs of change has already been covered earlier in connection with organizational design and management control. There is no need to repeat what has already been said. It is more important to concentrate upon one potential problem present in implementation of an operational control system: the risk of too much management commitment.

Development of an operational control system takes time. Premature implementation or product introduction involves far more risks than potential benefits.

New products, and the operational control systems which deliver them, generate excitement. Management tends to want everything done yesterday. The real risk, then, is that a management commitment can overrun the resources available for system implementation. There's an old saying covering this type of situation: "We always seem to have time to fix our mistakes, never enough to do things right in the first place."

We have seldom encountered a situation which justifies crash implementation of an operational control system. This is particularly true since the competitive advantages which trigger haste are seldom sufficient to justify the accompanying risks of failure. At best, competitive advantages through early introduction of a new product are temporary. Operational control systems are immediately apparent to and easily copied by competitors.

To illustrate, consider the CMA program at Merrill Lynch.

The exposure to competitive copying was obvious and apparent throughout the development of this new product. However, management recognized the value of quality sufficiently to approve a program in which the new product was introduced in four markets initially, then expanded from there. In the long run, customers who receive quality service will provide more permanent benefits than any transient gains from premature introduction.

Involvement

Again, points made in the two previous chapters about the need for and nature of involvement by those responsible for making a program work will not be repeated here. However, it is worth emphasizing that the implementation of an operational control system must be a line user activity. This job can't be done for the user by staff personnel. Staff people can coach or help. They can't do the actual implementation.

The point: if the user organization does not understand the system well enough to implement it, it will not understand it well enough to provide services to customers. The user organization and its delivery system are organically linked. They are a single entity. Implementation of a system cannot be separated from its users.

Phasing – Rate of Absorption of Change

If an operational control system has the right level of management commitment (without overcommitment or undercommitment), and if there is a high level of user involvement, the absorption capability for a new system is greatly enhanced. It may well be impossible to implement an operational control system in parallel – without requiring serial or phased implementation. Therefore, the extent of phasing appropriate for an operational control system will relate directly to the extent of user acceptance and readiness which have been developed. User readiness, in turn, can come only from an adequate level of involvement.

WHERE DOES THIS LEAD US NOW?

Capabilities for accepting and implementing programs for change within an organization center around the receptivity level of its people. The best plans and most insightful concepts lead nowhere if an organization won't accept or is not ready for the impact of change. Therefore, the steps necessary for the creation of an environment to accept and accommodate to change form the subject matter of the next chapter of this book.

10
THE REALITY
OF CHANGE

WHY IS CHANGE A PROBLEM?

Change has become an inevitable life process within our civilization. However, while people generally accept the inevitability of birth, taxes, and death, they tend to resist change. This has created a situation in which people's reactions to change reflect both fear and resistance.

Recognizing this, most of the content of this book has been about change – change in organizations, in management, and in systems. We have established that service companies compete through management policy and that implementation of policy requires continuous change – of varying degree and extent. Therefore, in the final analysis, it appears true that service entities compete also through their ability to accept and implement change.

Most literature dealing with change is concerned with such topics as the management of change or the accelerated rate of change. Most publications about change present impressive statistics on the dynamics of our current environment. These discussions imply, either purposely or inadvertently, that executives must do battle with change – that confrontation and conflict are inevitabilities of change. The reasoning follows that change is bad and must be conquered.

The obvious rationale behind such assumptions is that change is, by definition, different from what went before. People are asked to leave the familiar for the untried, possibly unproven. Resistance is understandable, if regrettable. In point of fact, we submit, change is a normal condition over which people have little or no control.

What can management do to instill a constructive attitude toward change?

Psychologists tell us that the resistance we observe against change results from the fears and frustrations of affected individuals. These feelings, in turn, apparently result from a sensation of anger.

The feelings of individuals were cited at the beginning of this book as keys to the need for a system of management for changing the way things are done in service enterprises. In these earlier references, the feelings covered were those of customers. Now it seems appropriate to come back to the topic of feelings of frustration, covering it this time from the vantage point of the provider of services.

The main issue to be addressed in considering the phenomenon of frustration and resulting anger is that anger is individual, not institutional. Therefore, the causes of anger must be addressed on an individual basis beginning with the frustrations faced by the individual who seeks to initiate change – the innovating manager.

If we as managers do not deal with frustrations over change as they relate to us, we will not be able to cope with the frustrations and anger of others. If we do recognize and deal with these elements personally, we are able to help other individuals within our organizations to accept the need for change. Once accepted, the prospect of change can generate a high degree of enthusiasm. This enthusiasm, in turn, generates tremendous quantities of competitive energy.

BUT HOW DO COMPANIES
COMPETE THROUGH CHANGE?

Companies compete by recognizing and assimilating into the culture of their organization the fact that change is normal and usually good. A competitive advantage accrues from treating change as an opportunity rather than something to be feared. When this happens, change becomes part of the organization's way of life.

This is illustrated effectively by looking at the competitive success enjoyed by Merrill Lynch. One of the key ingredients of this organization's success has been its attitude toward innovation. Merrill Lynch does not regard innovation as being confined to something brand new. It could be said that the company does *not* have a philosophy of being first – that the organization's history has been one of innovative following. A willingness to change is part of the fabric and disposition of the organization as a whole. At every organizational level, employees are conditioned to challenge ways in which products, services, or the entire distribution system may be better tailored to customer demands. This attitude, coupled with an entrepreneurial spirit to which the organization is dedicated, has created an environment which welcomes change. This philosophy, in the final analysis, has probably spawned Merrill Lynch's most competitive policy.

Interestingly, this policy has not been hoarded by Merrill Lynch management. It has not been treated as though it is a trade secret. Merrill Lynch executives discuss their policies openly, with full confidence that they cannot readily be copied. Competitors do not copy organizational feelings.

Results from the application of this philosophy have been legendary. While the investment banking community as a whole has tended to struggle to maintain the status quo, Merrill Lynch has continually diversified and expanded into areas traditionally served by other segments of the financial community. Today, Merrill Lynch has taken on the status of a full-service financial institution. The company now has major interests and offerings in insurance, real estate, employee relocation services, money management, economics, and commodities.

In the service sector, an understanding that people are the primary resource and that competition stems from people, not products, should lead to recognition that organizational security comes from competence and capability of people. If this realization can be internalized throughout an organization, feelings of fear and frustration, which lead to anger, can be dramatically diffused. In short, if an organization feels good about itself and competent in its capabilities, change is not a problem. The ability to deal with change, rather, becomes a competitive advantage.

WHAT IS THE PROCESS OF CHANGE?

The process of change is a process of communication. In our experience, communication is the most necessary, basic ingredient for effecting change. The communication required is of the simplest kind – people talking to each other openly and frankly. When this happens, frustration, fear, and anger are dissipated because there are no grounds for them. People become frustrated when they have a feeling of being left out, misunderstood, or uninvolved in what is happening to them. Open, honest communication dissipates these potential problems. We believe that most people have a positive disposition toward believing the best about things, not the worst. Communications processes within an organization should be oriented to capitalize on this phenomenon.

There is an old saying that bad news travels faster than good news. This can only be overcome by developing communications programs which transmit good news faster than bad.

We have encountered many situations where top managers attempting to invoke change have realized that many members of middle management had grown obsolete. These people were not "tracking" with new philosophies. We have observed, in most cases, that the fault does not lie with the middle managers, but at top levels. Executives have not taken the time to communicate what the new philosophy is. Thus, instead of an obsolete group of middle managers, the organization has a turned-off group, a group which resists change because change is not understood.

HOW DO YOU IMPLEMENT CHANGE?

We have said that change should be normal and that anger can be diffused through honest, open communication. It follows, then, that the final acceptance and implementation of change stems from the daily activities of the entire organization. Change is everybody's business.

If this kind of attitude is established, programs for change are continuous. Therefore, enthusiasm for change becomes a way of life, a habit.

A further result of such an attitude is recognition that all improvements, no matter how extensive, are only temporary at best. All changes generate problems of their own which, in turn, have to be solved through additional changes.

In summary, change begins with everybody and proceeds continuously. If this really happens, the working environment becomes one of enthusiasm. People have fun. Everybody wants success. Everybody believes that nothing succeeds like success. If such attitudes and beliefs can be nurtured and stimulated, a few successes, evenly shared, offset many failures (which should also be shared evenly).

World-class competitors who breed the will to win into service enterprises learn from successes; they do not bemoan their failures.

11
MAKING THE QUALITY-PRODUCTIVITY CONNECTION IN YOUR OWN ORGANIZATION

WHERE DOES THE CONNECTION START?

Throughout this book, the point has been made that the system of management presented is practical and proven. It works – partly because it has been put together from a series of established elements. But just how does it work?

In addressing this question, let's hypothesize a situation which occurs with some frequency for experienced management consultants: suppose a client with whom I had worked before calls to say he has taken on a new executive position, in an organization which he has just joined. Informally and conversationally, he asks: "If you were me, what would you do first to take hold of this situation? How would you assess what is needed? How would you identify opportunities?"

The first thing I would advise such a friend or client to do would be to resist the common temptation of feeling that he had to do something, anything. I have watched too many managers and executives move into jobs with a feeling that they had to start doing something – that action was demanded of them right away.

Frequently, executives tend to feel that their initiatives will produce effective results simply because the same things have worked well elsewhere. An executive coming into a new job may try something because it produced good results in his last position. Another individual may have observed or studied programs which have worked in other companies.

My point is that there is always an apparently valid reason for most executive actions. The problem is that many programs are launched without full consideration of their impact upon the specific organization or group of people who will be directly affected.

I have seen many executives frustrated on finding that results from short-term actions are exactly the opposite of those anticipated. This is because each group of individuals evolves its own personality or behavioral norms. These must be understood before being tampered with. An executive moving into a new position may find it far more effective to do little or nothing at the outset. The first step, I feel, lies in defining what constitutes success in each individual situation. Thus, my informal advice to a client or friend assuming a new position might well be: "The best thing to do right in the beginning is probably nothing. Use your start-up time to familiarize yourself with the organization and its culture. Think through your situation well enough so that you can define what success will look like for you and your organization."

The reason for waiting, and for thinking through changes before they are introduced, is largely because there are no problem-free solutions to anything. No matter how ideal a new approach may appear, it will, unquestionably, present a new set of problems in the course of implementation. We know the problems will be there. We just don't know what they are.

In approaching change, every executive should realize that, inevitably, one set of problems is being swapped for another. The problems with a current situation are at hand and known. The major requirement in planning for change is to seek the advice necessary to identify and anticipate those problems which will materialize in the future. By confronting them before they occur, it becomes possible, at least to some extent, to evaluate their magnitude and to plan to deal with them. This type of study enables the executive to decide which set of problems is preferable.

This, basically, is what my proposed system of management recommends: start by identifying the criteria for success. By success, I mean long-term success. In moving into a new position, every executive should be interested in the long pull, in success that will last and support growth. Temporary, cosmetic measures may be necessary. But you don't start with these. You begin by identifying what your organization will look like after you have made it successful.

If you are looking for really lasting success, the place you have to start is with management policy. Since service enterprises compete through management policy, success in a service undertaking requires a winning policy – one which establishes a direct connection between the quality of services rendered, as perceived by the customer or client, and the productivity of the people rendering those services. These policies should be incorporated in a statement which delineates the character of the organization and describes its basic beliefs in terms of a commitment to quality and to objectives for productivity. Such a statement should guide the entire organization in establishing a self-image with which it can identify. Management policies should become the personality of the organization. Virtually all other management actions should flow from traits fostered by policies.

WHAT DOES A WINNING SET OF POLICIES ACTUALLY LOOK LIKE?

What does this set of policies actually look like? Let's look at a real example. The following is a management policy statement I encountered recently at Salomon Brothers, the investment banking firm:

> Salomon Brothers articulates the following statements of policy:
> - People are the key.
> - No partners sit on the boards of public corporations.
> - We do not manage other people's money.
> - Our people are salaried, not on commission.
> - We manage no mutual funds.
> - Partners' profits and capital must remain in the firm.

This statement describes the culture and basic beliefs which guide the conduct of business at Salomon Brothers. Management believes these policies to be right for their organization. They may not be equally appropriate for any other firm in the investment banking industry. But, at Salomon Brothers, they provide the strategic directions which underlie the competitive success of that particular firm. They tell the financial community, partners, and employees of the firm what the company stands for. These policies establish guidelines for an environment within which business is transacted. All Salomon Brothers management plans and actions emanate from these policies.

To illustrate further, Touche Ross & Co. recently published and distributed to its management team a formal statement of personnel policy. It reads, in part:

1. The ability of our *average* partners and the average capability of our *best* partners compared to our competitors is probably the best measure of our firm's long-run competitive stance.

2. The development of people cannot occur effectively without conscious effort.

3. If people development is given high priority, all of the other firm objectives – growth, profit, quality of service, etc. – can and should occur if proper leadership, direction, and management are present.

4. People development is fundamentally a *line* activity carried on at the local-office level.

5. Primary responsibility for an individual's development necessarily rests with the individual; it is the firm's responsibility to provide the overall working environment, tools, experience, and guidance to support the individual's efforts.

6. On-the-job experience, together with effective guidance, provide an individual's primary sources of development. Formalized training programs are important adjuncts to the development process, but must be viewed as secondary to experience.

My own firm's personnel policy is significant because, in the public accounting profession, we regard people as our main resource and chief product. Thus, this policy enunciates a commitment to developing our key resource.

WHAT DO POLICIES DO FOR YOU?

Policies like those illustrated above present management challenges at different levels. On one level, there is a challenge in communicating the policies, in making them understood conceptually and intellectually.

Still another challenge lies in securing a commitment to the policies, even though this commitment may still be at a conceptual or intellectual level.

Then, an entirely different degree of challenge is encountered when it comes to implementing a set of policies and making it a living, breathing part of the operating life of the organization.

Before implementation can take place, policies must be internalized by the people who will live with them. The positions and actions presented must become a part of the behavioral norm of the organization as a whole. Implementation then becomes the key factor in a program for leadership which results in management success.

Implementing a set of policies requires consistency. The manager who enunciates a policy must live within it. This is critical. A manager cannot behave in a manner contrary to his or her own policies. Saying one thing and doing another only serves to confuse the organization. If a manager cannot communicate policies through personal actions, something is wrong with the policies.

WHAT FOLLOWS POLICIES?

Once an executive is satisfied with a set of policies and understands the necessity to operate within it at all times, the next level of implementation may proceed. Remember, this reference is to a system of management and means, therefore, that all of the elements have to dovetail.

The next level in the management system described in this book is strategic planning. How such plans are developed is not detailed chiefly because strategic planning is not viewed as a systematic, process-oriented activity. Instead, strategic plans are seen as results of irregular, intermittent management activities performed on the basis of need and opportunity, rather than schedules.

Strategic plans must be in place. Given policies like the ones illustrated above, I think of strategic plans as including three elements – objectives, goals, and management programs. These elements are identified as prerequisites. Then focus is on a system of management which takes its direction from strategic plans.

I consider objectives to be statements of purpose which are timeless, which are consistent with my business policies, and which can serve as guiding principles for the rest of my system of management. Within this same context, goals are interim statements of purpose or targets for accomplishment. Management programs, then, cover the things to be done immediately and in the short-range future.

Let me illustrate this with the situation of a major bank client. Management established an objective – which was seen as related to the bank's own quality-productivity connection – to shift market emphasis from consumer, or retail, services in the direction of corporate, or wholesale, services.

Goals derived from this objective covered the level and caliber of services to be provided to corporations, the relative profitability expected from each segment of the corporate marketplace, and the resources to be allocated.

Management programs were of a short-range, tactical nature. They concentrated on implementing the goals, largely by setting up market-oriented services. As one example, this bank established a corporate cash management network as one of the products to be promoted in changing business emphasis.

The key issue addressed with an integrated strategic plan of this type is that everyone responsible for achievement of any portion of the plan should understand where the motivation and direction come from. Because the cash management program is part of a set which includes high-level objectives and goals, all employees dealing with bank customers can operate with an understanding of the direction of the business and emphasis placed upon their jobs.

This caliber of understanding is important in a service enterprise because the employees who provide the service interact directly with – and in some cases function as partners of – the clients. Therefore, customers are affected directly by the attitudes of the people who serve them. Thus, the entire bank benefits when these people understand the purpose of what they are doing and can feel committed to and involved in the programs they are asked to implement.

WHO SHOULD DO STRATEGIC PLANNING?

My experiences have convinced me that, although strategic plans are necessary, they need not be highly formalized. What matters is that people understand where the organization is going and that those same people have been involved in some way in formulating strategic plans.

The most effective strategic planning programs I've seen or been involved with have been developed and implemented by ''line'' people within the organization. In saying this, I'm contrasting work by line, or operating, people with the efforts of planning professionals in staff positions.

In my opinion, the strategic planning which guided Citibank into becoming the largest financial institution in New York was successful because the people charged with delivering services were involved in planning for those services. Similarly, at Merrill Lynch, strategies were successful because the plans were put together by staff people who were knowledgeable enough to assume a line role in formulating and implementing new programs.

I'm not saying that staff people don't belong in strategy formulation. Staff planners have a necessary role to fulfill because many operating people don't have the time, the expertise, the discipline, or the objectivity to perform much of the analysis necessary to planning. Staff people must provide the necessary support. But if the plans are to be implemented successfully, it is necessary to have the participation and support of the people who will carry them out.

The logic behind the need to involve line people is, I believe, critical. Planning is a process for deciding what to do today to get where you want to be tomorrow. Planning is not really as future oriented as it is sometimes characterized. Plans must be built upon a detailed operating knowledge of today's situation, including current problems which must be addressed.

The value of this kind of dynamic approach to planning is well illustrated by pointing to companies that don't do it. Service enterprises which operate in a completely reactive mode can be seen all the time. Occasionally, this mode of operation is understandable, even desirable. However, if management can't or won't be objective enough to think about where the organization is going and can't or won't build a culture or basic philosophy by establishing a policy and purpose, then the long-range viability of the organization is questionable.

HOW DO YOU DESIGN AN ORGANIZATION TO IMPLEMENT STRATEGIC PLANS?

Plans are implemented through effective organizational design and leadership. Earlier chapters on this subject made it clear that the organizational design techniques recommended are of an off-the-shelf nature. A variety of design approaches is available and can be workable. Some combination of established principles is probably suitable to solve any manager's problem, in any situation.

No matter what approach is taken, I like to stress that the starting point for organizational design is the same for any entity. That is, each organization rendering services must be matched with its environment. Most successful companies have applied this principle. Its application led Citibank to the "minibank" concept described earlier.

The most common complaint I hear, either as a consultant serving clients or as a manager of a service enterprise, is that service isn't being rendered as it is supposed to be from the viewpoint of the customer. The clients don't feel they are important or that their needs are being considered in the way services are being rendered. When this happens, I submit, there is probably a flaw in organizational design.

Any type of service organization – be it a public accounting firm, a law firm, an insurance company, or a retailer – has to be organized to provide reliable client contact and continuity of service. The organizational design techniques or structures a company uses internally to support the rendering of service are less important than those where actual client contact takes place. The principle of client responsibility remains unchanged. It is a must. However, my experience has shown that this consideration often gets less attention and lower priorities than it deserves.

A commitment to client responsibility *is* the quality connection. Satisfaction which makes for quality stems directly from this relationship. Conversely also, the same relationship holds the key to productivity. A person fulfilling a client relationship feels a commitment to effective and efficient performance. This is because the same person is both deliverer and producer of services. There is quite a bit of difference between this kind of relationship and one in which a product or service is generated to be delivered by a third-party institution.

This stresses a point about organizational design made earlier: more can be done to assure quality of services and productivity in their delivery within the area of organizational design than in any other aspect of management.

I have seen this principle work. A dramatic case which I encountered personally in making the quality-productivity connection through organizational design involved a major provider of third-party coverage for group health insurance.

A study was undertaken because billing of employer organizations was logjammed and backlogged. Increasing numbers and dollar volumes of delinquent accounts were being reported from among blue-chip corporations which normally pay this type of bill promptly. These delinquencies, in turn, were inconveniencing the very employees who were supposed to be receiving benefits. When employee claims were processed through the reimbursement organization's computer system, delinquent status caused benefit payments to be held up. This was a major quality problem. People perceive quality health insurance as being hassle free. Problems with claims are problems with quality.

Analysis of this situation revealed that the group billing department was highly functionalized. All tasks were so specialized that no individual, even the department as a whole, had any feeling of customer relationship or responsibility. The problem was demonstrated by the titles of the people doing the work, including checkers, matchers, batchers, inquirers, and loggers. The flow of work between functions was batched and uneven. Tremendous backlogs developed between work stations. Costs of transaction processing were rising proportionately with volumes. In other words, experience showed that increasing volumes had no positive effect on productivity.

After examining several organizational design alternatives, including the straightforward addition of more people, it was decided to initiate a team approach, with specific groups of people identified with and responsible to individual corporate customers.

Implementation of a pilot, or test, group was carried out over one weekend. All files and other facilities necessary for operations were decentralized along team lines. The pilot team was, in effect, set up in its own shop. The idea was to impart a feeling that the team had its own property and exercised control over relationships with its own customers.

The team leader was placed in direct contact with specific corporate clients. Each team had enough staff and other resources to process billing for its customers – from beginning to end.

The operational controls essential for the processing stream within a functional organization were virtually eliminated because the small team processed entire transactions from input to completed bills.

After the problems associated with the solution were recognized and corrected, the remaining teams were implemented within a short time span.

A sense of service quality was instilled through the assignment of responsibilities. Productivity was enhanced by the elimination of functional controls and management redundancy. Teams started to compete with each other to eliminate backlogs and to improve group-billing productivity.

Within three months, the department was operating on a current basis. The backlog evaporated; customer complaints ceased. Cost reductions ran to nearly 50 percent a few months after the changeover. The quality-productivity connection had been made.

The same kind of quality-productivity connection was established during a program implemented in the trust department of a major money-center bank. The problem was similar to the one experienced by the health-care reimbursement agency.

Quality of service had diminished to a level where the president of the bank had written a personal letter to the customers of the trust department assuring them that the bank would be financially responsible for any losses or tax consequences suffered because of delays or oversights in processing transactions.

The department, which was only marginally profitable, was bogged down in functional, technically-oriented processing organized according to type of transaction. Functional examples of job titles included trust openings, trust closings, securities buys, securities sells, reporting, and account reconciliations. Morale within the department was low. People felt overburdened by processing workloads.

There was no satisfaction because the fragmented approach to processing left no room for the building of client relationships. Further, there was no incentive for productivity. There was also no responsibility established for getting a day's work done in any given day. Under the functional approach, an attitude developed which held that whatever didn't get done today could always be processed tomorrow.

Internal coordination problems were reaching serious levels within the bank. The trust function was sufficiently different from mainstream banking and credit functions so that line executives felt helpless to do anything about the problem. All they knew was that the trust department was a sore spot in customer relations and a potential blight on the bank's image.

The preliminary study of this operation served to establish that there was, in fact, a potential for patterns of client relationship and responsibility. A series of teams were established around specific types of trusts. Each type of trust equated to a classification of customers. The newly formed teams were given the personnel, the responsibility, and the authority to carry transactions through from beginning to end for their own group of customers. These teams represented the bank completely in trust services – from setting up initial agreements to follow-through in processing transactions and delivering results to trust clients. Even marketing responsibility was incorporated within these new teams.

As team members experienced success under the new system, satisfaction and pride grew. Personnel extended themselves to do even more, to do a better job.

As functional ''hand-offs'' between processing steps were

eliminated, the need for controls to monitor each step of the process was also eliminated. Fewer people accomplished more. This was reflected in a cost reduction of approximately 30 percent for the department as a whole.

Over a period of six months, customer complaints dwindled from a steady flow to virtually zero. The exposure for reimbursing client losses was eliminated. Profitability of the entire trust operation was increased.

WHAT SHOULD BE DONE
ABOUT MANAGEMENT CONTROL?

On assuming a new responsibility, among the first questions I would encourage an executive to ask would be:

- What resources am I responsible for?
- What information do I need to manage those resources?

I'm talking now about management control. The kind of information I feel is required to manage resources is current and future oriented. Such information does not normally flow from a financial reporting system. Financial reporting is essential. But it isn't the same as, and doesn't replace, management information dealing with the allocation and use of resources.

As I think about the cross section of executives I have observed over the years, I recall people who have come to their positions knowing what business they wanted to be in. They have done a creative job, by and large, of organizing to conduct their businesses successfully. As a class, the executives I have seen have almost totally overlooked the need for management controls to monitor implementation of the plans they have drawn so carefully. It is almost a case of people not knowing what they don't know. Important questions never get asked.

The point is that competitive success is achieved through a total system of management. Success requires a continuity which includes policies, plans, organizational design, management control, and operational control. Any break in this chain endangers the prospects of competitive success. In our experience, a frequently missing link is management control.

This is not to imply a lack of conscientious effort by managers. Quite to the contrary, the managers we see are extremely diligent as a group. The problem, rather, is that many businesses are being managed at the wrong level. There seems to be an assumption that once plans and organizational design are in place, the business can be managed at the operating level. This results in situations where top managers are involved in transactions and day-to-day events, rather than in managing the resources of the business. This is a particularly common failing among executives who have grown up through the ranks of their existing organizations. Such people seem to revert to the things they know best – the functional operations which gave them their start.

The situation of the department store chain described earlier illustrates this phenomenon very well. Management control became a missing link. When this happened, the operations of the organization ran completely out of alignment with organizational design. For practical purposes, management was no longer in the business they thought they were in. Operations assumed a kind of identity of their own. When something of this type happens, management finds out about it, too often, only when customer complaints become too loud to ignore.

We ran into the same type of situation experienced by management of the department store in a large financial institution. This enterprise had organized itself around its customer base. An effective pattern of customer relations had been established. Operations had been designed to support the departmental teams which were established.

Management didn't know there was a quality problem until customer complaints came to their attention. Analysis showed that the operating systems were not under reliable control. In this particular situation, quality control measurement was based on upward reporting on a functional basis from the operational control system. Reports were in terms of number of transactions improperly handled as a percentage of total transactions handled. This measurement of quality control was effective and adequate as an operational control. However, there was a dimension missing for evaluating quality at the management level.

The missing ingredient in this case was a management report covering the value of mishandled transactions in terms of dollars, as compared with total dollars processed. This, the situation proved, is the way customers look at their transactions. Had management controls reported transaction processing errors on this basis, management would have developed a far more acute sensitivity for customer problems than was possible on a purely volume basis.

The problem, here as elsewhere, lay in a failure to recognize the differences in characteristics between operating and management controls. Operating controls report on a bottom-up basis while management control is a top-down process. Management control is the link between plans and organizational design at the top and operations at the customer-contact level. If management information is missing, operations can run out of control for extended periods without detection.

Another great danger in implementing management control – and we have seen this often as well – is that the development of management controls may be delegated to technical experts who insist on building the operating controls and data bases first. They get around to management controls only after these operational controls and data bases are designed fully. This doesn't work. At minimum, I believe it necessary that management controls and operating controls be developed together, on a coordinated basis. Wherever feasible, I think it best to establish the needs of management control before technical functions are specified. Operational control should take direction from and provide information to management control, not the other way around.

When management control is missing, the quality-productivity connection is broken. Quality can deteriorate without management cognizance.

I saw a situation not long ago where missing management controls damaged productivity. My firm was called in to look at the operational efficiency of a large life insurance company which prides itself on its image for outstanding quality of services. The company has set itself apart from its competitors by offering exceptionally high levels of service.

The examination showed that costs had been relatively ignored in management's quest for quality – carried out through the existing organizational design. The review showed that the quality objectives were being met. But they were being met at the expense of productivity. The quality commitment was increasing costs. Without offsetting increases in productivity or flexibility in pricing, profitability declined.

Within this company, there were no management controls in place to show that profits were, in fact, being eroded in the quest for quality. Management never asked: "How much service improvement can we afford?" Instead, the question tended to be: "How much service can we provide to keep building our image?"

An effective set of management controls could have established a perspective on how much service could have been provided without overburdening costs. Examples of problems which emerged because management controls were missing included:

- A system for budgeting and profit planning at the departmental level – which should have been almost second nature in an organization of this type – was missing.
- Product-line, or service, profit-contribution measurement was also missing. Management had no way of telling what each line of business was contributing to the company.
- Management didn't know their earnings until after year-end financial closings.

Operating controls within this organization were first class. We also found planning and organizational design to be adequate. The missing link was management control. In this situation, productivity suffered. The quality-productivity connection had been broken this time because productivity suffered at the expense of quality.

HOW CAN YOU MAKE AN
OPERATIONAL CONTROL SYSTEM WORK?

Operational control systems almost always work. They work because they have to. How efficiently or effectively they work is another question. That's where I believe executives should direct their attention and energy.

Most of the effective operational control systems I have seen have been those in which the users were so closely involved that they felt a proprietorship over them. Each user felt he or she was the driving force causing the system to operate. The user did not feel forced to work under an impersonal system. An effective and efficient operational control system is looked on as a tool by the people using it. The system belongs to its users.

I am not talking about some sort of abstract ideal or anarchy where everybody does his or her own thing. I am, however, convinced that it is possible to have an automated or mechanized tool installed while actually preserving or enhancing the feeling of pride and of client relationship among people delivering services. Pride and sensitivity can be just as much a part of a system which incorporates automated processing as they are in a so-called, old-fashioned cottage industry.

The point is that automated equipment and systems have their place today. No knowledge worker in our post-industrial society really wants to perform tasks which are considered beneath the dignity, skills, or even interest, of the individual. People don't get excited about doing jobs that are described in terms of batching, matching, or checking.

In the case of the health-care reimbursement organization, these jobs were imposed upon workers by an inherently bad system. When the system was changed to permit people to use their judgment and skills, things improved.

Therefore, when I talk about a user being an integral part of an operational control system, I am not visualizing a situation in which all work is done manually by a team of happy people. Rather, my reference envisions situations in which mechanical work best handled by machines is automated to relieve the drudgery imposed upon the people. Workers do the things for which they are best suited – exercising judgment and interacting with other people.

By the same token, when I talk about decentralization and distribution of operational controls, this is often misunderstood to imply complete decentralization of all operations – with a minicomputer at every desk. This is an extreme. In the real world, extremes don't work. I don't believe in trying to impose systems at either extreme of the centralization-decentralization spectrum, any more than I would advocate any other extreme position. It is far more workable to find a sensible balance, decentralizing only those things which benefit from this treatment.

To illustrate the kind of balance I'm talking about between centralization and decentralization, let's look back at the "minibanks" set up by Citibank. The driving force here was a desire to bring people rendering services – and the complete services themselves – into closer contact with customers. However, there was no way that management of Citibank could expect the Federal Reserve and the New York Clearing House to interact with them at multiple locations just because the bank had decided to decentralize its operations. The practical solution involved setting up an operational control system which served as a shared resource through which the "minibanks" were connected with the Federal Reserve and the clearing house.

In the case of the health-care reimbursement agency cited earlier, the automated aspects of the operational control system were centralized in a huge, data-base-oriented computer system. However, members of the customer-oriented teams were provided with direct access to that system – at their own discretion rather than under control of the data processing function. Responsibility for the accuracy of the data base rested with the team, not with the central function or some kind of anonymous "black box."

For an executive taking over a new position, a major concern in the operational control area would be to avoid being lulled simply by the fact that the existing system worked. The operational control system should be challenged in terms of how well it makes the quality-productivity connection. This is the place where the connection is most frequently broken.

The management system I've been talking about is a sequence. Organizational design has to come first. Management control has to be developed. But, if operational control doesn't conform to these other elements of the overall management system, there can be no final payoff in quality, productivity, and profitability. Operational controls must mesh with the other elements of the management system. Information must flow upward as well as downward. If this integration doesn't take place, the operational controls will eventually limit the kind of products or services an organization can offer in its marketplace.

I pointed out earlier that the operational control system is both the product and the process for its delivery. Thus, if operational controls are inflexible or archaic, they will inhibit the ability to change existing services or to introduce new ones. Operational controls become a limiting factor rather than a means of implementation.

I recently encountered a situation where this occurred in a large life insurance organization. Management plans and organizational design were innovative and far ahead of the capabilities of an old, outdated operational control system. A situation had actually arisen where the organization could plan and market new services a lot faster than it was able to deliver them. The operational control system had become weak because, as new services had been added, new operational processes had simply been tacked onto old systems. The entire operating mechanism had become weakened. Delivery capabilities were inhibited to a point where the company was unable to make the quality-productivity connection effectively and efficiently.

This is where the integrated management system I have been talking about comes full circle. If planning and implementation for organizational design and management control have been effective and efficient, quality, productivity, and profitability are delivered by the operational control system.

I, too, seem to have come full circle. I appear to have returned to the original question: What does a world-class competitor look like among service organizations?

It is probably true in any sector that long-term competitive success stems from the performance of people. Through my own experiences, however, I have become convinced that people failures will drag a successful organization down faster than product failures. Further, service entities will suffer more from people failures than product-related organizations. This is not to say that people are not important to product-oriented companies. They are. But people-related problems will pull a service organization down faster than they will a company with established products.

This dependence upon and vulnerability to people among

service organizations brings both good news and bad news to managers in the service sector. Let's look at the good news first: once management realizes that people and the policies responsible for their development hold the key to competitive success, the search for apparent short-term solutions may be abandoned.

Now for the bad news: implementing championship policies requires changes in attitude and behavior. It is impossible, however, to change attitude and behavior directly. This must be accomplished through changes in the environment within which people operate. Changing the environment, in turn, is a time-consuming, extremely complex, and often frustrating process for an action-oriented, results-seeking executive.

As I see it, then, the real issue facing service sector managers is to stimulate people to do two things:

1. People generally, and managers in particular, have to recognize that change must begin in themselves before they can realize change in others. It is considerably easier to change yourself than someone else. Therefore, the place to start is obvious. Professor Anthony Athos of the Harvard Business School, has an effective way of phrasing this: "You are part of the problem you are trying to solve."

2. Management must realize that people perform far better when they do things they believe in – as opposed to things that management concludes are right for them. When people take actions implementing their own decisions, even at the lowest operating levels, they produce results with little or no management effort. On the other hand, if people are implementing conclusions handed down by someone else, an elaborate scheme of control is necessary to assure implementation.

My feeling in this matter is that winning ways stem from championship attitudes. William James summed up this situation extremely well by writing: "The great discovery of my generation is that man can change his circumstances by changing his attitude."

INDEX